7 LAWS OF TRUE PROSPERITY

CECIL KEMP

HARVEST HOUSE PUBLISHERS
EUGENE, OREGON

Published in association with George D. Williams, gdavidwilliams@bellsouth.net.

Cover design by Dugan Design Group, Minneapolis, Minnesota

7 LAWS OF TRUE PROSPERITY
Previously published as *7 Laws of Highest Prosperity*
Copyright © 2001 by Cecil O. Kemp Jr.
Published 2013 by Harvest House Publishers
Eugene, Oregon 97402
www.harvesthousepublishers.com

Library of Congress Cataloging-in-Publication Data

Kemp, Cecil.
7 laws of true prosperity / Cecil Kemp.
    p. cm.
Rev. ed. of: 7 laws of highest prosperity : making your life count for what really counts.
    ©2001.
ISBN 978-0-7369-5331-3 (pbk.)
ISBN 978-0-7369-5332-0 (eBook)
1. Success—Religious aspects—Christianity. 2. Success. 3. Conduct of life. 4. Self-actualization (Psychology)—Religious aspects—Christianity. 5. Self-actualization (Psychology) 6. Wealth—Religious aspects—Christianity. 7. Wealth. 8. Spiritual life. I. Kemp, Cecil. 7 laws of highest prosperity. II. Title. III. Title: Seven laws of true prosperity.
BV4598.3K46 2013
248.4—dc23

                                                                        2012026075

Printed in the United States of America

        13 14 15 16 17 18 19 20 / BP-JH/ 10 9 8 7 6 5 4 3 2 1

To my beautiful wife, Patty.
Thank you for your incomparable love,
your constant encouragement, and
your inspiring, godly example of what it means to be
a Proverbs 31 wife and mother.
It is my honor and privilege to be your husband.

Acknowledgments

Highest thanks to Father God, Jesus, and the Holy Spirit.

Readers, I'm so glad you picked up this book. My prayer is that it will instruct, challenge, inspire, and help empower you to live a truly difference-making life of genuine significance.

Special thanks to my parents and my wife's parents: Cecil and Peggy Kemp and Hermon and Frances Robertson; to our children, Heather and Rusty; and to our grandchildren, Justus, Jessi, Briley, and Abby.

Thank you Ms. Clara Millican and Ms. Dora Medaris. You were my wife's and my closest spiritual mentors.

I want to thank Harvest House Publishers and its wonderful staff.

I'd also like to thank Kathryn Knight, George Williams, Wes Yoder, Ron Miller, Diana Donovan, and many other contributing, creative individuals who believed in me and this book's message.

Contents

God's laws are perfect.
They protect us, make us wise, and
    give us joy and light.
God's laws are pure, eternal, just.
They are more desirable than gold.
They are sweeter than honey
    dripping from a honeycomb.
For they warn us away from harm and
    give success to those who obey them.

PSALM 19:7-11

A Prosperity Parable

In 1923, a very important meeting took place in Chicago. Of this high-powered group of people who knew the secrets of making money, nine were the most financially successful people in the world at that time. Where were these nine people twenty-five years later? Six knew how to make a lot of money, but they failed to really prosper because they didn't live by the "7 laws of true prosperity." Of these six, the great wheat speculator died abroad and insolvent. The president of one of the largest independent steel companies died bankrupt, having lived on borrowed money for the last five years of his life. The president of a large utility company was a fugitive from justice and died penniless in a foreign land. The member of the United States' presidential cabinet was pardoned and released from prison, only to die at home shortly thereafter. The president of the New York Stock Exchange was in prison. And the president of a successful gas company was deemed insane.

The other three individuals chose to live by the 7 laws of true prosperity. Consequently, they remained materially wealthy and genuinely prosperous.

Which example do you want to follow? The path to true prosperity, I'm sure. And that's what this parable is designed to help you do.

I hope you enjoy getting to know Sam the wood gatherer. As you follow his story, you'll discover some guiding principles about life, wealth, and true riches that can change and enhance your world. And when you're finished reading, I pray you'll choose to embrace the laws of true prosperity so you too can experience all a life walking with the Lord offers...a life that counts for what's really important and leaves a positive imprint on every person you touch.

1

The Restless Voice

Sam the wood gatherer was a young man—a rather simple man who came from a family of wood gatherers who, in turn, came from families of wood gatherers. They lived in a village with more good people who had a simple approach to life. They worked very hard to maintain their station in life because, indeed, maintaining one's station can be very hard work, can it not?

And perhaps this is why the village folk found it odd that Sam was a questioning sort of young man. They didn't understand why he was always wondering about things. "Why do the lords of the realm live in great houses made of brick?" Sam asked. "And why do we gather wood all day from the forest floor to sell to the townsfolk yet have so little left to fuel our own hearth fires?" Sam even asked, "Why is there so little joy in our lives? After all, don't we work very hard and dedicate ourselves to our tasks?"

One woman, bent double from carrying bundles of wood all her life, finally growled, "The lords live in great homes because they have wealth. We are not destined to be rich. We are to keep to ourselves and be happy with what we have."

"But you're not happy, Magda," replied Sam. "You groan under each load you carry. And I've heard you long for the delicious fruits the townsfolk eat and envy their music festivals and dancing."

"I'm very happy!" snapped Magda. "I know my place. I can live just fine without the apples and pears and music of the town." And she returned to her work, grumbling under her breath.

Every day Sam gathered wood and tried to ignore his curiosity, his doubts, and the longings of his heart.

Until one day…

The buyer of wood from the nearest town became ill and couldn't come to the village to purchase and pick up firewood. Several young men from the village, including Sam, were sent on the long trek through the forest to the town, their backs laden with huge bundles of wood. The walk was arduous, and Sam couldn't help but wonder why the village didn't own a cart.

When they reached the marketplace, the town square was bustling with activity. The humble village men stood to one side, the wood piled neatly next to them. They waited for someone to come over to buy their firewood. But the people gathered around the other merchants selling goods. Brick sellers, paper sellers, fruit sellers, wheat sellers—all were loudly and happily extolling the excellence of their products.

Taking note, young Sam spoke up. "If anyone needs good firewood, find it here! We offer the very best firewood from the forest."

Sam's companions stared at him. "Hush!" warned one man. "We are merely simple folk who offer twigs and branches. Show not pride, for we are but village dwellers—"

"How much is your wood?" interrupted a well-dressed gentleman in green woolen clothes. He stepped closer and leaned toward Sam.

"We receive two farthings a cord from the buyer who visits our village. This is the price we offer to you."

"Two farthings? What a bargain for the 'very best firewood.' I'll buy the lot."

And so the forest dwellers returned home, happy with their sale but weary from the journey. The next day they were so tired they gathered very little wood. They didn't have much to carry to the town, which was necessary because the town buyer wasn't yet well enough to travel.

Again the young men stood in the town square. And again Sam called out, "If anyone needs good firewood, find it here! The very best firewood from the forest."

Promptly the same gentleman in the sporty green clothes stepped over. But this time he took Sam aside and spoke to him in a soft voice. "I will buy all your wood again at two farthings a cord, but now I know why it is so cheap. Other firewood sells for six farthings a cord, but it burns well into the night. This wood you sell is partially rotted from being on the forest floor so long. It will burn, but it does so very quickly and with much smoke. Tell me, do you not find it so for your own fires?"

Sam thought for a moment. "Yes, you're right," he admitted. "It burns much too quickly. We are constantly feeding our fires to keep warm. Our fire tenders are kept busy day and night."

"So you agree this is not the *best* firewood from the forest?"

"Perhaps not," replied Sam. "But we work so very, very hard all day to gather it…"

"But you agree this is not the *very best* firewood from the forest?" the man repeated.

Sam quietly said, "I guess I do agree."

The man, as he promised, bought every bit of wood, which provided just enough money for the men to buy the food the villagers needed.

All the way home, Sam lagged behind, deep in thought and wondering why his spirit felt so burdened.

2

A Determined Heart

That evening Sam's heart was heavy, but he said little to his family or fellow villagers. Instead, he mulled over the words of the gentleman who had purchased all the firewood.

The next morning as the men and women went about their daily tasks, Sam and his wood-gathering companion headed into the woods. Sam decided to bring up what he'd been thinking about.

"We always gather the easiest wood to find and carry, yes?" Sam asked the older man.

"Of course."

"Why is that so?"

"Because it's always been done this way. Our work is so labor intensive that we would be foolish to go further than necessary to find wood or to lug back the largest pieces of fallen wood in the forest. How our backs would ache then!"

"But we remain so poor. Perhaps we're poor because we offer low-quality firewood," suggested Sam.

The work partner abruptly stopped and glared at Sam. "Are you insulting the hard work the people in our village do?"

"I simply—"

"Are you demeaning our efforts?"

"No, no! Not at all," Sam said hurriedly. "I was just thinking that our great efforts could be put to better use. Perhaps we could—"

"Perhaps we can stop talking nonsense and continue our work. Who are we to question the ways that have always been? Do we not have enough to buy what the village needs? Does not the bread man bring enough food each day in his cart? Do we not have adequate shelter in our huts even though they're made with twigs and mud? Do we not have each other so we can share our…our…"

"Misery?" offered Sam.

His fellow wood gatherer stood up straight—well, as straight as his crooked back would allow. He stared angrily off into the trees. Then he turned to Sam. "We may be poor. We may even be miserable. But we are people who work hard. I am proud of the work I do. My exhaustion at the end of the day is a mark of my contributions to my family and village. You would do best to take pride in the work you do, young man. Now, let's get back to gathering wood."

Sam returned to work and considered what his co-laborer had said. He thought about what the townsman had said about the quality of the firewood. He contemplated what his heart was feeling. *I will!* he said to himself. *From this day on, I will do my best and take pride in my work.*

Around mid afternoon, the wood gatherers brought their day's work to the village center. People were hunched over as they carried their heavy loads of twigs and branches and then dropped them to form a large pile. Again the wood would be divvied up between the men who would carry it to town. The pile wasn't as large as usual because the younger gatherers were worn out from walking to town and back each day to sell what was gathered. The gatherers hoped there was enough wood to provide enough food for the village.

A joyful whistling coming from the forest caught everyone's attention. They turned their heads and watched as Sam entered the clearing. He was heavy-laden with a few large branches and two cracked logs of oak. He placed them at the edge of the pile and smiled.

"You fool!" cried a villager. "You have gathered fewer pieces than the others. You've been lazy in your work."

Still smiling, Sam responded gently, "No, good woman. I have not been lazy. I've brought the very best wood I could find. I had to travel through the forest until I found what I was looking for—a windbreak with trees that were dead but still standing, located not far from the king's new road. See these fine pieces? They'll burn well! I've worked hard and traveled far, and my legs and back are quite weary indeed."

"But you were whistling!" accused another.

Sam nodded. "My legs are weary, but my heart is light. Today I've done my best so I can offer the townspeople the highest quality firewood available."

The villagers weren't sure how to respond. Muttering, they went straight to the task of loading up the men who were walking to town. Sam shouldered his portion, and the men set off. Although the others complained about their heavy loads and the long walk, Sam moved along without a groan.

At the marketplace, they sold their wood quickly. Sam was happy, indeed, as he watched the same well-dressed gentleman in green hand over six farthings for his firewood. And when the young men returned home, Sam didn't gloat or smirk at the other wood gatherers. His heart swelled with pride when he unobtrusively handed the extra four farthings to the merchant the next day for additional food for everyone in the village.

Sam attended to his work diligently, happy and whistling. And life continued that way.

Until one day…

The recovered wood buyer once again brought his cart to the forest village to purchase and transport the firewood. The villagers were delighted, to say the least, for their wood-gathering efforts had been sorely diminished because the young men had to make the long, weary walk to town every day. In fact, had it not been for the extra farthings Sam's fine firewood garnered, some of the villagers might have gone hungry.

So everyone was relieved the wood buyer was back at work— except Sam. He'd come to relish the sights and sounds of the town. He loved to see the smiling faces of the potters, the apple sellers, the mothers and their plump, healthy children. He took in every detail around him—the sturdy homes made of fine split logs and sunbaked bricks; the smartly styled wool clothing dyed green, blue, red, or yellow worn by the wealthiest townspeople; and the well-appointed storefronts of thriving businesses. The prosperity amazed young Sam, and carrying his hard-won load of wood to town was barely noticeable as he anticipated arriving at the marketplace.

But the wood buyer was healthy, so all the wood gatherers in the village were back to their regular work schedule of many hours spent gathering wood…and more hours of gathering wood…and even more hours of gathering wood. Sam continued to gather his firewood at the spot where he'd found long-dead trees leaning against each other. Because they were off the ground, they were dry but not rotted.

Sam was proud of his newly developed agility that came from working his way along large limbs to harvest thick branches. He was proud of his sharpened ability to spot pieces of limbs that had fallen and cracked but were still perfect for firewood. He was proud to offer his fine wood to the wood buyer and receive six farthings every time.

Because he was doing his best and being diligent in his work, Sam figured he should be happy. And on the surface he was. But deep in his heart was a longing he didn't understand. Something was missing, but he didn't know what it was.

What he didn't realize was that God was putting the hours and hours of wood gathering to good use by planting dreams. During those many long mornings and long afternoons, Sam began to imagine what life would be like if change was allowed.

3

Let the Dreams Begin!

The long, tedious days of a wood gatherer rarely brought satisfaction or understanding. One day ran into the next with numbing monotony that robbed the soul, mind, and body of joy, beauty, and hope. And because this was so, the villagers dealt with their flat existence with a self-imposed resignation that this was how their lives were meant to be.

To dare to think about bettering their lot would be an admission of failure at best and greed at worst. Did they not have enough bread? Did their work not serve three purposes—to provide a living for them, to clear the woods of rotted wood, and to supply the town with an economical source of fuel? And weren't they better off than the beggars in town or the people who labored inside dingy rooms all day? Surely even the wealthy land barons had their miseries. And so faithfully each evening the villagers prayed, saying thank you to God for providing the wood that sustained their lives. But since his "awakening" to the desire to do his very best, Sam's prayers had changed. "Thank You, God, for showing me where the best wood is and giving me the strength to carry it to the village. Thank You for the extra money it brings so there is more food for the people."

And Sam's days were a bit different too. Each day he returned from his work laden with wood but whistling merrily. And each morning he arose eager to do his work. Not only was the forest offering good firewood, it was also giving Sam solace and the time to truly listen to the sounds around him and the dreams God was planting in his heart.

All day he daydreamed about saving a wee bit from his earnings so he could buy a cart. How grand that would be! With a cart, two men could haul the wood to town each day, and surely the wood buyer would pay the village a bit extra if the wood was delivered! And with the cart, the men could pick up food for the village, saving money because the goods wouldn't have a delivery charge. And perhaps, just perhaps, there would be others who would be willing to gather the best wood with him, and the village could earn enough for some special treats, such as fresh fruit. And perhaps the villagers could even work fewer hours and have some time and energy to spend some evenings singing and maybe even dancing around a community campfire. Then the people would have smiles on their faces, and the children would laugh and play.

Sam loved his days filled with spirited dreams even though he was working long and hard so he was exhausted by the end of the day. But when he shared his joy and his dreams with his friends and co-workers, he only got blank stares or disdainful looks in return.

"You have time to spend your days dreaming?" one man said. "Perhaps you aren't working hard enough!"

"A cart, he says! A cart that will need mending. A cart that will get stuck in the mud on rainy days. Let the townspeople bother with carts. Let them deal with the problems of repairing and maintaining them. And let them come to us. Why should we make their lives easier by delivering the wood?"

"You want us to go deeper into the woods and learn to shinny up trunks to get branches when it's much easier to gather branches from the forest floor? And what if we did climb up the trees? Wouldn't we fall and break our backs? Then where would we be?"

Sam responded as calmly as he could. "You won't fall. I'll show the younger workers how to climb up and cut the branches off so the older workers can sort them for hauling to the village. We could get a good supply in less time if we worked together. And though the distance is more, the weight of the wood is less because it is drier than what we've been gathering. If all our wood were that dry, the town buyer would pay more for it because it would be the *best* firewood, which is what the townsfolk truly want..."

"*Townsfolk* want! *They* want? Why do we care what *they* want? Are we their servants? If we take the wood to them each day, they'll get used to it and always expect it. And there's no guarantee they'll pay more. Are you on our side or theirs?"

"Are we not bound together as a village?" Sam started.

"*You* seem to be bound to *them*," a village elder interrupted. "The townspeople care nothing for us. They see us as poor wood gatherers. Why should we bend over backward to please them?"

Sam turned away and went back to his work, thinking, *Because they see us as poor wood gatherers...*

And so it was that Sam continued his days as a wood gatherer. Although he kept his dreams and hopes locked inside, his heart overflowed with faith and inspiration. God filled his eyes with visions of a better life—a happier, satisfying life full of joy. A life with more celebration and little drudgery.

Until one day...

Sam was suddenly struck with an idea that seemed to come by divine inspiration. He'd been praying earnestly and wistfully as he searched for the best wood, climbed the dead trees, slid to the ends of limbs, cut the branches, gathered what dropped to the ground, and then stacked the wood for ease in loading up to carry to the village. "God, You created all the wonders in this forest. Surely You wish more happiness for Your children. Yet we seem to be stuck. What could be worse than thanklessly gathering wood all day only to live in poverty with no joy? Oh how I yearn for a better life for my fellow villagers and me. But they only scoff. Please help me, Lord," he implored.

And then the thought hit him with such truth and weight that he stood stunned. He dropped the wood he was carrying. There was indeed something worse than economical poverty. There was something worse than ridicule. There was something infinitely worse. It was to dream…to listen to his heart while it communed with the Holy Spirit…and then not act on what God was encouraging and challenging him to do. In that moment Sam knew his life could not—would not—be constrained by the limitations of the villagers. God had a plan for him…to prosper him in every life dimension!

The next day Sam did something unusual. He packed a small bag of clothes, hefted a load of his very fine firewood onto his back, and said goodbye to the villagers who gathered to witness this rare occurrence. As the men and women shook their heads in disapproval, Sam ignored their frowns. Instead he set off whistling with God's dream in his heart.

4
Building a New Life

So Sam became a townsman. He arrived at the marketplace tired but happy. His fine wood earned eight farthings this time. After selling the wood to the gentleman in the fine green coat, he asked him where he might find suitable lodgings and work. Because Sam was honest and had shown a willingness to learn, the wealthy businessman said he'd be glad to help. "Until you find your own place, you're welcome to stay with my hired hands in the comfortable quarters I provide at the stables. I'll talk to a construction foreman I know to see if he has a job available."

"Thank you," Sam replied. "I'm willing to work hard and do my best!"

"Why don't we meet back here in two hours. I'll finish my business and then show you the way to the stables."

"That sounds great!" Sam said. "That gives me a chance to explore the town a bit."

So the businessman set off to finish his workday. Sam headed down main street to check out the stores and get a feel for how the townspeople lived. Two hours later, the two men met again in the town square.

"I have good news!" the businessman declared. "I've met with Grecco, an excellent construction foreman who builds homes, and he says he's willing to give you an entry-level opportunity. He has an opening and says you can start tomorrow."

"I appreciate this! I won't let you down."

And with that, the two men headed to the businessman's home. Sam settled into the hired hand quarters in the stables, and the next morning, bright and early, he was up and raring to go. He arrived at the town square early, looking forward to meeting the foreman.

When Grecco arrived, Sam introduced himself. After talking briefly, the two men shook hands and walked to the construction site. After providing a quick overview of the work, Grecco said, "I'm glad you're on board, Sam. I'm sure you'll do fine." He turned Sam over to the man in charge of timber before going about his own work.

Sam's first job was hauling felled trees to be cut into timber for building. He was grateful and felt truly blessed to be of service—to earn his keep and apply the knowledge he knew about wood gathering. He worked diligently and honestly, whistling through the day and sleeping soundly at night. He soon saved enough to sign a lease for a small, comfortable apartment on the second floor of the carriage house owned by the head mason.

Sam learned as much as possible from his fellow workers, and his keen sense of observation and reasoning impressed his supervisor and Grecco. Sam devised a strong cart with two wheels that allowed several logs to be hauled faster and by fewer men. He encouraged the planting of new trees to replace the ones they felled, showing foresight and concern for the coming generations. He also volunteered after work, helping the less fortunate build huts and storage sheds.

Within a year, Grecco asked Sam to work with the framing crew on projects involving larger homes and prominent business establishments.

"That would be great, sir," responded Sam. "But I have little work experience on framing, stonework, and masonry. I'm eager to become an apprentice, but—"

"You will be perfect!" announced Grecco. "Since you admit you know little, we can teach you the correct way to do these things from the beginning."

And so they did.

Sam was grateful, happy, and hopeful. His eyes were opened to a new line of work and a new way of life. He was in awe of the grand homes and buildings that took shape under Grecco's careful oversight. The little houses on the outskirts of town were left behind, and the littler huts in Sam's forest village seemed even more distant.

Now a respected member of this large and bustling town, Sam soon met a wonderful seamstress well known for the quality of her work. After a suitable courtship, Sam proposed, and the lovely Suzette said yes! Sam felt loved and blessed. When Suzette moved into the small apartment above the carriage house, Sam promised that within two years they would have a home of their own.

Together the young couple dreamed about their own home— a cozy cottage in the market area. Suzette envisioned a room in front with a big window where she could sew, embroider, and welcome customers. They dreamed of a comfortable, warm place with lovely things to lift their spirits and fine friends and food to feed their souls and bodies. They looked forward to hearing the pitter-patter of their children's feet running down the hall.

Then one day…

A member of the crew Sam worked with purchased a small house. Jealousy whispered into Sam's ear, "If he can afford a house, why can't you? You and Suzette deserve one more than he does." That insidious thought crept into Sam's mind and grew. Soon the dreams and joy God had planted in his heart were obscured by the haze of jealousy and envy. The desire to get his own house *now* hit Sam hard. *This fellow does the same work I do, and he bought a house!* he thought. *If he can do it, I can. Besides, Suzette and I deserve our own place more than he does.*

Sam ignored the fact that his coworker relied on financial help from his parents and a brother. Overriding Suzette's concerns, Sam decided they would borrow money so they could get a house right away. It would be nicer than the one the crewman had purchased. That was only fitting, after all, because Sam worked long and hard. Though it would stretch their budget and require him to work even more hours, Sam was sure they could handle it. "When everyone sees how well we're doing, I'm sure it will bring in new business," he told Suzette. "Success breeds success."

That sounded good, but the truth is that no matter how blessed people are, many want more for the sake of having more. They long for what others have whether they can afford it or not. That seems to be part of the human condition. Once the "me too" bug bites, infection comes gradually, slowly filling the mind and heart with dissatisfaction.

And Sam was no exception. After he moved into their new place, he enjoyed getting the house up to the right standard. Noticing his neighbor had a new yard cart, Sam went out and purchased one with lots more bells and whistles. When his other neighbor built a brand-new deck, Sam built a nicer one.

Fortunately for Sam, his excellent work earned him a promotion to foreman over his own crew. Delighted, he now had the authority to instruct his crew to pay more attention to details, to be more efficient, and to consider the special details that new homeowners would appreciate. As his crew's reputation for integrity and innovation grew, the demand for their work increased in the area and, eventually, throughout the kingdom. The additional income eased the burden Sam and Suzette felt from their house mortgage loan and maintaining a more expensive lifestyle.

Eleven years after Sam moved to town and six years after he became a foreman, he and Suzette were living very comfortably in their upper-middle class neighborhood. They had three wonderful children and seemed to be the perfect family. True, Sam was rarely home to enjoy his family and cozy home. He was busy accepting every large job offered. He and his crew worked hard and long to take advantage of the boom in business.

Sam's outward wealth seemed to increase, and his circle of friends expanded to include well-off clients and many prominent businesspeople. Sam's inward riches, however, decreased as his time spent with God decreased and gradually disappeared. His appetites for more possessions and status grew. When Grecco, who had bought the construction company, showed up at a meeting in a new suit, Sam immediately ordered a similar one. When he noticed the mayor had a brand-new black carriage, Sam vowed to own one like it within three years. Each time he saw the mayor's new vehicle, Sam's desire grew. Finally he could stand it no longer. He borrowed the needed funds and purchased a more ornate carriage only six months later.

Socializing with his wealthy clients, Sam soon discovered they often invested in businesses other than their own. At first he felt left out, unknowledgeable, and insecure. Falling behind his friends wasn't an option, so Sam sought their advice and looked for more opportunities to make a financial killing. After all, he knew he was smart, ambitious, and entitled to every advantage available. When an investment didn't pan out, he quickly grabbed onto the next one, hoping to make enough to compensate for the previous loss plus get ahead.

Suzette's days were filled with raising their children and caring for their household. She continued her seamstress work part-time, offering her customers quality at a reasonable price. With growing anxiety, she watched as her Sam grew more agitated, distant, and penny-pinching each day. She noticed he no longer whistled on his way to and from work. He criticized the amount she spent on household expenses and groceries. And she'd heard that his crewman were grumbling about the long hours and the demands placed on them. They no longer enjoyed working for Sam. Some left to work on other crews even knowing they would earn less pay.

When Sam came home one day and announced they were moving into a large brick house on Miller Street, Suzette knew she was expected to be excited about the grander house and taking the next step up the social ladder. But she wasn't. "How can we afford such a large house?" she asked. "And why do we need such a big place for just five of us?"

"How can we afford not to!" Sam replied. "Surely the best construction foreman in the kingdom should live in a house worthy of his reputation. If I want to be more successful, I need to look successful! Just think how prosperous people will think we are when we live on Miller Street. It will be good for business."

After the move, Sam and Suzette did indeed look prosperous. But as the bills mounted, Sam's anxiety grew. He took on more and more work, rushing his crew through each contract so they could start bigger projects. If quality suffered a little, that was okay, Sam decided. Even his crew's less-than-best work was better than the work done by other crews. He ignored the pleadings of his workers to slow down and take more time on each project. He refused to consider implementing the little extras homeowners appreciated because they required more time and money.

When Suzette questioned what he was doing and the hours he was working, Sam turned to his new friends for advice. He no longer had time to carefully consider the advice he received or to pray about his decisions before investing. Soon he was losing money right and left. His business suffered, his peace of mind suffered, and his family suffered.

A year after the move to Miller Street, Sam was on the brink of ruin. With only one signed contract, he had time on his hands instead of work. One by one the best men on his crew had quit, so Sam had been forced to hire workers who did barely enough to get by. They were an unhappy lot, and the lack of work didn't help.

Fear of failing consumed Sam. He drove his crew hard, but himself even harder. He snapped at Suzette and barricaded himself in his study when he got home. He desperately searched for opportunities to quickly get back the prosperity he'd enjoyed. He was sure if he could get one more loan, he and his crew could get by until business picked up. After all, the downturn in business wasn't his fault. He'd done his best to keep his crew busy. He'd been on top before, and he would be on top again.

Then one day...

Sam was walking down the street when an older gentleman paused next to him.

"Why, aren't you Sam, the wood gatherer from the village in the forest?" the old man inquired jauntily.

"Yes. Yes, I am," Sam replied distractedly, his thoughts abruptly pulled away from his financial woes.

"You are doing well, I presume?"

"Very well," replied Sam automatically.

The older gentlemen studied his face. "I can tell you aren't happy, my man. I remember how you used to always whistle while walking down the street. What's wrong? Are you ill? Has something happened in your family?"

A bit aggravated, Sam responded, "No one is ill. My family is fine. Sure, I've had some recent business setbacks, and I'm between job contracts right now, but I'm determined to succeed. I'll be on top again in no time. Nothing and no one will deny me the financial success I deserve."

The older gentlemen contemplated Sam, observing his demeanor with an even keener eye. "You wish prosperity, Sam?"

"Of course! Doesn't everyone?"

"I suppose so," replied the old gentleman. He reflected for a moment. "But very few know what it is and how to claim it, don't you agree?"

"*Claim* it? Don't you mean earn it?" Sam replied. "I've worked hard and put in long hours for my successes. And they will come again!" Sam stopped and stared at the man. "Say, I know you. Menro, isn't it? We haven't talked for a long time…" Embarrassment for saying so much hit Sam, and his voice trailed off while his gaze hit the ground.

"I can help you, Sam," the gentleman stated with quiet authority.

Sam looked up and noticed the old man's steady-but-kind gaze.

Menro added, "I always believed you were destined for something special…"

"I'll get my money back. I know I can do it!" Sam interrupted. "I can recoup my losses. I'm on my way to see Geoffrey the moneylender right now. With one more loan I'm sure I can get ahead again. Then my family and I will once again be on top of the world and able to enjoy the best money can buy."

"Ah, you are truly in earnest," Menro said gently. He paused. "Sam, I can help you if you'll—"

"Have you become a moneylender?" Sam cut in.

"No…"

"Are you friends with the moneylender?"

"Not friends, no."

Sam was cautious. How many times had he heard business associates, customers, and vendors say "I can help you," only to learn they were bent on helping themselves no matter what it cost others?

"Sam, I do know someone who knows the moneylender's dealings inside and out. I'm sure my friend would be willing to advise you regarding success. If anyone can help you realize your goal of prosperity, I believe Magowin can. Yes…yes. In fact, the more I think of it, the more I know you really must stop by and talk with him. You can't miss his shop. Magowin is the shoemaker on Dairy Street, three shops this side of the moneylender's place."

Sam's pent-up anxieties, hopes, and desperation burst out in a fit of laughter. "A cobbler? Oh yes, Menro," Sam said. "I will certainly consult a cobbler."

"Why not talk to him, Sam? What can it hurt? I'm sure he can help you. Tell him I sent you." Patting Sam firmly on the shoulder, Menro went on his way down the cobblestone street.

"Now I'm late!" muttered Sam. He walked to the corner and turned onto Dairy Street. He passed the shoemaker's shop and headed straight to Geoffrey the moneylender's establishment. A sign on the door read: Closed for the Day.

"Now what!" Sam exclaimed. After a few minutes of pacing and venting his frustration, Sam determined that he would find the moneylender to plead his case. But where to start? Then he remembered the old gentleman's words. "I know someone who knows the moneylender's dealings inside and out…" Magowin the cobbler! He might know where Geoffrey is.

And so Sam found himself at the door of the tiny cobbler's shop. When he entered, Magowin was working while whistling a merry tune.

5
Soul Searching

Looking up, the cobbler called to Sam, "Come in, my good man! Ah, you look like a man whose soles need mending, yes?"

Sam looked across a wooden bench strewn with every sort of foot apparel imaginable—from sandals to leather work boots, from elegant beaded dancing shoes to carved wooden clogs. Then he looked up into the azure eyes of a whiskered, bespectacled, smiling, old cobbler.

"Er, no..." Sam felt a bit self-conscious. *If Magowin does know the moneylender well, I'd better make a good impression,* he thought. "No, sir," he said more brightly. "Actually, I'm here to see if you might know where I can find Geoffrey the moneylender. I need to talk to him today. It's important. It concerns...a...a cousin who is in sad straits. You see—" Sam cleared his throat. "So you see, I need to find him. Menro suggested you might be able to help me."

"Ah, Menro!" Magowin leaned his head back and laughed heartily. "A man who stays with the same pair of shoes for ten years. Can you imagine? For ten years! Not good for my business, no, but we are good friends. Yes, good friends." The cobbler put down the pink leather slipper he was working on and looked squarely into Sam's worry-lined face. "But you don't care about that I'm sure, young man. Come, sit over here and tell me why you seek this moneylender."

Feeling out of place but having nowhere else to turn, Sam moved to the one vacant chair and sat down. He discovered he was relieved to sink into it. The cobbler's shop was pleasant indeed, in a warm sort of way. It smelled of leather and wood shavings and, perhaps, a hint of freshly baked bread.

"So you do know where Geoffrey is?" asked Sam in earnest.

"I know. Yes, I know. And you're right. I know him quite well. We've had discussions, yes, many discussions on finance. I really enjoy teaching financial strategies."

"You?" Sam questioned before quickly realizing his comment was out of line. "W–what I mean, sir, is that—"

"It's quite all right, my good man. Quite all right. You see, though I earn a simple living making shoes and mending soles, I've found great contentment, satisfaction, and prosperity. I've discovered a set of seven laws or principles that lead to genuine success and happiness. I'm delighted to share these, and I've taught many men and women who were willing to listen to and implement these laws. You might say I'm in the happiness business."

Sam leaned forward. "What do you teach?"

"How to attain true prosperity." The cobbler casually reached into his pocket, pulled out two ripe plums, and handed one to Sam. "Care to join me?"

In all his days Sam couldn't remember experiencing such a strange encounter, such an odd moment, such a curious circumstance as this. Here he was in a small cobbler shop, sitting in a worn-but-comfortable chair, biting into a ripe plum, wondering what was going to come next, and suddenly realizing he was more relaxed than he'd been in a long time. There was something very unreal about the situation, yet something very real and familiar.

Sam snapped out of his reverie and responded to Magowin's

comment. "True prosperity? What do you mean you teach how to attain it? Where do you teach? Are you wealthy then?"

"Hmmm, some people would say I'm well off," said Magowin, casually picking up the pink leather slipper he'd been working on. "Where do I teach? I teach here in my shop. I teach on the street. I teach wherever I meet people willing to learn. Are you looking for a teacher?" Magowin asked casually, his gaze focused on the slipper in his hand.

Sam squirmed in his chair. "No, I'm looking for Geoffrey the moneylender."

"May I ask why, my good man?"

Sam was surprised to find himself responding to the man's obvious sincerity by being honest. "I need to borrow money so my family and I can stay in our home. I just need some extra cash until business picks up again. It's a temporary loan, you see. Actually…" Sam chuckled a bit drily. "Actually I'm a prosperous man myself. Times are just a bit hard right now. I was misled into making some bad investments, and other foremen enticed the best men on my crew to work for them. I've had picky clients, demanding vendors, and workers who aren't skilled enough or quick enough to get the jobs done right and on time. But I know I can turn my business around with just a little financial help…" Sam's gaze wandered to the people strolling by the window.

"I see," Magowin replied calmly while working on the slipper. "Well, I'm glad you're doing well. I only teach prosperous people."

Sam did a quick double take. "What do you mean you only teach prosperous people? Why do they need teaching if they're already prosperous?" Sam realized he was no longer at ease in the little shop. He stood. "Anyway, I don't need a teacher. I know how to be successful. I did it once; I can do it again. I just need to find Geoffrey. He's the one I need. Do you know where he is?"

Magowin put the slipper down and faced Sam. The truth he

spoke next struck deep into Sam's heart. "No, Sam. You don't need Geoffrey the moneylender. He won't help you now. You owe him too much already, and he can't help you out of the calamitous situation you're in. What you need is already available to you. You must simply trust and claim it.

"What you need is to celebrate the prosperity that already belongs to you. You need to rediscover how to whistle. You need to understand what real success is all about. What you need, Sam, is to learn and follow the seven laws that lead to contentment, fulfillment, and true prosperity."

Sam stood, mouth agape. He stared at this odd, little man with whiskers who seemed to know so much about his situation. Finally he shook his head slightly and found himself asking, "Will you teach me?"

"But of course!" Magowin came around the counter and slapped his visitor on the back. After laughing heartily, he said, "I thought you'd never ask. Come back tomorrow at two o'clock. We'll begin then. And while we talk, you can help me with my work. Fair enough?"

"Yes. Two o'clock. I'll be here," Sam confirmed.

Magowin walked Sam to the door, his hand resting on the younger man's shoulder. "Wonderful! One more thing. I have a homework assignment for you. Before we meet, I want you to review your life, answering these questions." For emphasis, Magowin held up his right hand and used his fingers to check off each question. "How did your family make a living when you were growing up? What did they teach you about money? What makes you happy when you work? Let's see now, I know there were a couple more. Oh, yes! What attracted you to your wife? And what goes through your head when you think about work, saving, giving, and spending?

"Then I want you to prioritize your needs. And prioritize your values." Magowin continued as though this was just a simple assignment. "Address these questions too: What values did you learn as a child that have affected your views on money and success? What values do you intend to teach your children? How much do you include your wife in financial decision making? How do you define success? What's the source of your contentment? What's the source of your discontentment? What are your good habits, and what are your bad habits?" Magowin peered at Sam over his tiny spectacles. "And who are you really, Sam? Why do you want to be prosperous?"

"Wait, wait!" cried Sam, overwhelmed with this deluge. "I'll be up all night if I try to answer all those questions!"

"What a wonderful answer!" exclaimed Magowin. "I'm so glad you didn't say this assignment can't be done at all." He embraced Sam lightly. Returning to the area behind his workbench, he added, "You'd best get started, Sam. See you at two o'clock tomorrow."

Sam was halfway home when it occurred to him that he'd never told Magowin his name. Obviously the old cobbler knew him. Yes, the old man certainly knew him...

6

The Heart of the Matter

"Magowin the cobbler?" Suzette repeated.

Sam waited about thirty seconds before answering.

"Yes, Magowin the cobbler. I'm going to meet with him tomorrow at two o'clock to discuss a plan to…well, I suppose, to revive my business and pay for this house and—"

"It's just that—"

"I know, I know. He's a shoemaker. I was surprised too. I can't really explain how or why it came about, but I'm going to meet with him about business. And I think I'm even supposed to help him fix shoes while I'm there. That's even stranger!" At this Sam felt his smile creep across his face as he sensed—and enjoyed—the humor in what he was trying to explain…or, rather, not explain.

"N–n–no," Suzette stammered, "it's just that I can't believe… Or rather…I—I—I don't know what to say."

"It does sound silly, doesn't it?" Sam admitted. "But I promise, I'll just oblige him this once—"

"No, you're not understanding!"

Sam suddenly realized that Suzette's eyes were filled with tears.

"What you don't understand, Sam, is that for two years I've been asked on many occasions to sew clothes and coats for the people living on the outskirts of town," Suzette explained. "And each time

41

it's been *Magowin* who has commissioned the clothes and paid for every article. Once a month he collects the clothes and takes them, along with several pairs of shoes he's made or repaired, to the little stone church just past the market. Every month he comes whistling and smiling. And every month I wonder how he can afford to pay for so many clothes. I don't charge him full price because I know the clothes go to the needy, but still it's so much money for a cobbler.

"And the other day when you announced you were going to take out another loan, I found myself close to tears. And after you left I cried and prayed for hours. I prayed that we could find a better way to live and work. A way to pay our bills that doesn't include such misery. And I asked God to bless us with the abundance and happiness I see in Magowin every month. And now you come home and say you're going to meet with him. And you're going to help him make shoes. Sam, this is the most wonderful news I've heard since you asked me to marry you."

"Magowin does that?" Sam asked. "And you prayed for the same abundance and happiness you see in him?"

Suzette nodded.

Sam walked over to Suzette, and they embraced for a long time. No words were necessary.

So Sam entered the little cobbler shop a second time. This time he walked in with a lighter step, with the blessing of his wife, and with great hope in his heart.

"Two o'clock! Right on time. Punctuality is a virtue, Sam. So we know we're not starting with an empty slate, eh?" Magowin smiled as he greeted Sam. Then the cobbler plopped a stack of heavy, fragrant leather into Sam's arms before directing him to the workbench.

"Well, yes, right," responded Sam, eager to discover the secrets to recovering his wealth.

"Have a seat, Sam. You've cut leather before, yes?"

"Actually, a long time ago in the village where I grew up, we—"

"Wonderful! Here are the patterns to follow," Magowin cut in.

And with that Sam was immediately set to work on ten pairs of brown-leather house shoes.

Magowin's activities—cutting, stitching, tanning, helping customers by taking orders and writing up sales—provided the satisfying rhythm of a happy craftsman at work.

At five o'clock, during a quiet lull and after he'd cut out the last of the soles for the house shoes, Sam felt compelled to speak. "Magowin, in just three short hours I've learned much about your trade. But when are we going to discuss how to make money?"

"Never."

Sam stopped, confused. "Never?"

"Never. But we can begin the first lesson on achieving *true prosperity* right now."

"Oh…right," Sam said with hesitation.

"Right!" echoed Magowin with enthusiasm. "The first thing you need to do is kneel with me now. You can put those tools and leather to the side there. Come, kneel with me here. Together we'll praise God for the great riches in your life."

Sam realized that he might very well remain in a state of agreeable confusion as long as Magowin was his teacher. "Praise for what?" he asked. "I can't do that, Magowin. First of all, I'm so in debt and in need of work that I can't possibly praise God for any riches. I don't have any. And…and I'm ashamed I've failed, so I can't pray right now. Later, when I've—"

"But, my dear Sam," Magowin interrupted, his voice quiet and serious, "I told you I only teach prosperous people. Are you telling me you're not prosperous?"

"Well, I've *been* very prosperous. And I will be again because I'm determined to succeed. I've just got to! But right now…"

"Until you know how rich you already are, I can't help you, Sam."

"Forgive me, Magowin, but I don't understand. And please don't give up on me. My wife, Suzette, she was happier this morning than I've seen her in years because I was going to meet with you. I can't go home and tell her you won't teach me."

"Ah, your wife. She means a great deal to you. And your children?"

"Oh Magowin, Suzette is more than I deserve. And my children are a delight, but I credit my wife for their rearing. Without Suzette I would surely be a poor man…"

"I see. I have compassion for your plight, Sam. But I can't alter what's needed to teach you. Please go home and don't return until you are a prosperous man."

"Magowin, what are you saying?"

"I'm saying, my dear fellow, that you will never understand true prosperity until you feel worthy of the abundance in your life. And you will not feel worthy until you claim the riches around you and within you—and then dedicate those blessings to the One who gave them to you."

Sam, dumbfounded, got up and left the shop. He walked home slowly, wondering what he would tell Suzette. His thoughts went back to the night before when he'd worked on all the questions Magowin had given him. *Was all that work in vain?*

The next morning Sam was back at Magowin's shop. "Magowin, I am blessed! You were so right! I have so much to be thankful for. I have a loving wife, fascinating children, and a beautiful home. I have fine clothes and one of the best carriages in town. I am thankful for all I have, so I know I need to work even harder to keep my abundance. Now will you teach me?"

Magowin looked up with a benevolent smile. "You have been thinking, Sam. I can tell that. But you have not been *feeling*. No, Sam, we may not begin yet. The riches you name aren't eternal. If you lost your home and clothes and carriage, would you feel destitute?"

"Yes, I would," acknowledged Sam.

"If you were to find yourself alone for a year or more—without your loving wife and children—would you feel like a man with abundance?"

"Indeed not! How could I?" exclaimed Sam. "It would be horrible!"

"Then you must experience and claim that which fills your life with meaning and worth and which will endure no matter what."

The confused and depressed construction foreman left the cobbler's shop and headed home. The chill in the air reminded him that it was time to stock up on firewood for the coming winter. *How can I afford to buy wood this year?* he wondered. His remaining work contract and Suzette's sewing work wouldn't bring in enough money for the mortgage, the food, the household expenses, and firewood. *I'll have to gather my own wood,* thought Sam as shame and defeat filled his heart.

When he arrived home, he greeted Suzette with a weary smile. He told her quietly that after checking on his crew, he would spend the rest of the day gathering the firewood they'd need for the winter.

He hitched up his horse to one of his two work carts. After swinging by the construction site, he headed to the woods—to the old, familiar area of his youth. This was where he'd accepted Jesus as his Savior and experienced Holy Spirit-inspired dreams. And it was where, apparently, he was still the only one willing to make the long trip to gather dry wood. Sam set about gathering the locust and oak branches that hadn't started to rot.

The first half hour of gathering wood was depressing, but within the next hour Sam's heart felt less burdened. He soon realized he was enjoying the solitude and simplicity of the task at hand. He gave thanks for the sharp saw he hadn't had when he was younger. With this saw he could attack the thicker tree limbs. After the third hour of work, Sam was astonished to find that he was whistling. *Whistling! What had Magowin said about that?* Sam paused until the words came. *Yes! He said I need to rediscover how to whistle.*

In this quiet forest Sam suddenly felt at peace, free of the daily cares and duties that usually were his constant companions. He thought back to the last time when he'd felt such peace. With a small laugh he pictured the young Sam who had left his village with great dreams and feelings of self-worth and abundance filling his heart. *Feelings of being worthy of abundance. So I have felt that way before,* he decided with some astonishment. *Why did I feel that way? And how did I lose that feeling?*

Sam searched his mind and tried to come up with a way to put himself in that place again. He soon became frustrated and impatient because no solutions came. Finally he called out, "O God, won't You help me?" His cry reverberated through the trees and bounced back through the sunlight filtering around the whispering leaves.

And then wisdom came. Sam knelt down and pressed his hands to his face for quite a while. Words eventually poured out like liquid gold:

> *Dear God, I used to talk with You every day when I lived in the village. You were the source of my energy and the source of my comfort. I talked to You, and I listened as You talked to me. When You told me it was time to leave my home and begin a new path, I followed Your leading to use my talents and discover more joy in life. And I did. I really did!*

*But somewhere along the way I forgot You. And now
I'm in another kind of forest—a forest filled with
enticements, falsehoods, greed, and the desire to have
others look up to me. I'm sorry, Lord. Please forgive me. With Your help, I can change. Thank You
for Your willingness to love me and guide me. I want
to find the happiness I once knew in You. I see now
how blessed I am just to be Your creation. And I'm so
blessed to be married to Suzette and have our beautiful children to love.*

*God, I thank You with all my heart and all my soul.
My eyes, ears, and heart are again open to Your teachings. I want Your leadership and the great abundance
only You can provide. Amen.*

With true peace filling his heart, Sam finished loading his wood and made his way home. He unloaded most of the firewood, stacking it in the woodshed. He went inside and greeted Suzette with an embrace that said, "I'm happy, I'm home, and I love you."

The next day Sam opened the cobbler's shop door with little fanfare. When Magowin looked up, Sam quietly said, "Magowin, forgive me for interrupting your work, but I have a favor to ask of you. Will you help me deliver some firewood? I gathered it yesterday, and it's in my cart outside. Suzette and I very much wish to give it to someone who needs it. We hope you will know the best family to give it to. Will you help?"

Magowin put down his work, grabbed his coat, and closed up his shop without a word. Outside he nodded to Sam as they walked to the hitching post. They climbed onto the wooden seat in the wagon, and Magowin directed Sam to a small house just at the edge of town.

"Drive around the house, Sam. We can stack the wood there."

Quickly and quietly the two men unloaded and stacked the wood close to the house. They left without speaking to the woman and children they occasionally glimpsed as they passed by a window. On the way back, Magowin spoke. "That was kind of you and Suzette to share your wood."

"It wasn't out of kindness," Sam admitted. "It was out of thankfulness. God has given me so much that I wanted to thank Him. And when I shared that with Suzette, she wanted to give God her thanks too. I used to be a praying man, Magowin. I used to commune with God every day. He filled my heart with dreams and hope. Then I stopped. I'm not sure why or how or when, but I did.

"And then yesterday while I was out gathering wood, I remembered what I used to have. I asked God to forgive me, and I told Him I wanted to reclaim the wonder of that relationship. That I wanted to once again feel that it is enough just to walk with Him— living by His laws, doing what I love with the gifts He gave me, and providing the best I can to my customers. And God's peace again filled my heart. I am so thankful, Magowin. And I want to keep this feeling so much that I ache inside. My greatest fear is that I will stray from God again."

Just as he finished, they arrived in front of Magowin's shop. The older gentleman put his arm around Sam's shoulder. "Here we are, Sam. Let's go in. I have some stitching for you to do."

"But, Magowin, you said not to come back until I was prosperous."

"Do you claim God's love and grace?"

"Yes. With all my heart."

"Do you know in your heart that this love and grace will endure forever?"

"I do know this," said Sam. "What amazing gifts from God."

"Do you know that God and His love and grace are the true sources of your dreams, talents, and wealth?"

"They are. I'm absolutely sure about this, Magowin."

"Then you have embraced wisdom, Sam. You have entered the door that leads to fulfillment. You are claiming the riches of God's wisdom, and God will empower you to live an honorable life that can't be measured by mere gold. God's love gives you a real hope that radiates from your heart and will reach everyone you meet. You are a rich man, Sam. You are very prosperous."

"But how do I hold on to this feeling and this knowing? I am but a human with many faults and a heart that falters."

"You speak with wisdom, Sam. And we'll cover those issues during our lessons. For now, let's celebrate your great riches by stitching some house shoes."

7

A Spiritual Foundation

Magowin and Sam stitched ten pairs of slip-on house shoes that afternoon. They worked with some whistling, some wincing over pricked fingers, some laughing, some grumbling, and some good-natured comparisons of stitching techniques.

"You are a spiritual man, Magowin," Sam reflected during a quiet moment.

"Are we not all spiritual?" asked Magowin while closely inspecting some of Sam's stitching.

"Well, what I mean… What I'm wondering… What I'm trying to ask…Well, how have you remained so…so…"

Magowin looked up. "On track?"

Sam laughed. "Yes! I guess that's what I mean."

"I choose to."

Sam stopped mid-stitch. "Choose? But everyone who chooses to live honorably and according to God's wisdom doesn't keep in touch with God and His goodness."

"You're right, Sam. People may *want* to be honorable, but they don't always make a conscious and heartfelt decision to *choose* to be so all the time. I have chosen to allow God's wisdom and truth to guide my decisions and to frame my decisions within His priority structure. This leads to true freedom and genuine success, which makes a difference and lasts. If you remember, I mentioned following a set of principles or laws. There are seven of them. The first two laws are like a set of doors that open to the path of true prosperity. These two doors are set in the spiritual realm, but together they lead to success defined by God's principles here in the material world as well—"

"Wait! You've lost me, Magowin," Sam interrupted. "I want to make sure I understand this."

The old cobbler laughed. "Sometimes I lose myself!" And then Magowin began the discussion Sam had been craving.

"The first two laws, as I said, are like two doors. They are the spiritual laws that you must accept and live by to walk the path to true fulfillment. The first door is the *Law of Wisdom.* That means claiming and believing that God, the Divine and the Creator, is the ultimate source of wisdom and truth.

"The second door is the *Law of Priority.* This is accepting that your human priority list can't and won't serve you well. You enter this door—this law—when you accept that your priorities must be inspired by God's plan for your life and be heartfelt. This acceptance, of course, doesn't mean your human mind may not rebel at first."

Magowin paused to smile.

"That is why this is a spiritual law. The Law of Priority is an *act of faith and surrender* to the priorities God reveals to us in every facet of life.

"These two doors can only be entered when your heart is dedicated to God and you are open to speaking *and* listening to Him."

"Magowin, please help me understand this Law of Priority." Sam moved the leather shoe parts aside and concentrated on Magowin's face. "Is it not enough that I want...that *I choose*...to live a prayerful life in communion with the Creator?"

"Keep stitching, Sam. You will be helping me greatly if we can have those shoes ready by tomorrow."

"Okay," Sam said, pulling the materials back in front of him. "It's just that I thought the lesson was underway, and I wanted to concentrate on what you were teaching."

"These lessons you must learn with your heart. And your heart must be free to accept the truth within the lesson. And I've discovered that our hearts are most free during productive work."

Sam resumed stitching.

"To answer your question, Sam, you can enjoy a blessed life with God by retreating into the woods and living as a hermit. But tell me, when you were in the forest and you felt the desire to return to grace and clarity of purpose, were you resting quietly?"

"Oh my. No, I was working very hard gathering and loading wood."

"Ah, what a blessing work is, yes? You see, Sam, we are beings created for work, and we find our greatest happiness and worth when we live with God's wisdom active in our daily life of work, family, and community. And yes, even in the drudgery of life."

Sam sighed. "Magowin, this might seem easy for you, but this daily business you describe and my need to excel at work is what took my mind and heart away from living a simple life of faith."

Magowin looked at Sam with sincere understanding. "I know, Sam. I know your concern and your fear. I know this second law can seem to loom like an impossible entryway."

Pausing for a few seconds, the cobbler's azure eyes looked toward the wall. Sam decided Magowin was probably lost in some kind of memory.

"That is why this is also a door that requires faith," Magowin finally said. "It is not enough to just experience the spiritual power of God and accept that His wisdom is supreme. If that were enough, most people would be blissfully happy. But God created us in His image, Sam. That is why we are creative beings filled with passions, drives, desires, the need to work and produce, and the desire to love."

Magowin turned toward Sam. "Do you know where we tend to go wrong? We associate the human part of life with the physical only. We don't take our spiritual commitment into our daily life, we don't let our spiritual commitment influence or impact what we do in our day-to-day lives. Sam, was it really work and duty and family and life in general that kept you away from God? Or could it be that it didn't occur to you to take God and His wisdom with you every morning when you arose to go about your day—when you negotiated contracts and worked with your crew, when you spent time with your family, and when you attended to the daily chores?"

Sam nodded slowly.

"Priorities, Sam. They are so important. Without establishing godly priorities, we are locked out of achieving true prosperity. We can have a beautiful spiritual connection to God when we walk in the woods, but if that is the only time and place we talk to God, we'll not live fully in Him. Our lives will not be truly significant."

"I want to walk with God all the time, and I want my life to be significant. I'm thankful He's willing to work through me to reveal His love and mercy to the people I meet!" Sam declared.

"Good, Sam! Commit your heart and your entire life to living by God's priorities. The Divine Creator will not lead you astray. But it's not enough to *intellectually* proclaim that this is how you will live." Magowin tapped Sam on the forehead and then placed his palm on Sam's chest. "You must *feel* in your heart using faith. You must know and feel that God loves you enough to direct you in your work…in His work…in the work you do together. He wants you to help Him, Sam, and you really need Him."

Sam was inspired and feeling hopeful. "How do I know these priorities?"

"The first is clear. Love and honor God and listen to His wisdom. Make the Law of Wisdom your foundation. With faith pray for guidance that He will lead you. Live knowing that He is beside you always—He will never leave you or forsake you. He will place you in circumstances that enable you to get on track—His track—if you ask Him to and listen with your heart and maintain a dialog with Him."

"I'm still not sure about the feeling part. I *know* intellectually you're right, but…"

"You must *feel* with solid conviction that following God is the only way to true happiness. You must feel to your core that you want to live God's priorities. You need to believe in your heart that if you don't prioritize what you think about, what you attend to, what you pray for, and what you value according to God's principles and wisdom, your life will be utterly miserable. Experiencing God is not an ethereal, wispy feeling of oneness with the universe," Magowin said, sweeping his hand through the air with a dramatic flourish. "He's an active, vigorous part of our daily life. He's involved in everything we do and what we choose to create. And when He creates through us, we produce more than we dream possible. Doesn't this make you want to regroup and prioritize God's way, Sam?"

Sam nodded vigorously.

"Wonderful! Go home and share your heart with Suzette. Explain what we've talked about. Then together, and it's very important that you do it together, prioritize everything you can think of. Include how you spend your time, what warrants disciplinary action with your children, assuming they misbehave at times—"

"Oh, yes," Sam interjected.

Magowin smiled. "Also include what your expenditures should be and where and how you want to spend your time and energy."

"How will we know what God's priorities are?"

"Before you start, pray. Ask God for His wisdom and guidance.

And search the Bible regularly to discover His priorities for every life dimension. You might not get it down perfect the first time, but that's okay. This is the beginning of your journey. As you work on this, you'll realize more and more that you can't do it on your own. That you need God's help."

"Will we discuss knowing God's will more next time we meet? And are we going to talk about all those questions you asked me to think about when I first met you?"

"Ah! You have asked the right question at precisely the right time! I thoroughly enjoy noticing when the Creator is orchestrating my teaching." Magowin's face broke into a gleeful smile. "You and Suzette are to discuss those questions. You'll understand why as you talk. The answers will help you know where you've come from so you can know what you want to change to reprioritize and get where you want to go."

"When will we meet again? What will the next lesson cover?"

"You will learn the third law, but I won't be your teacher."

"What do you mean?"

"Your instructor on the third law might surprise you. She'll teach you as soon as your ears are open so you will understand the truth of her words. She's an expert on this third law, and you would be wise to heed her authority."

"Who is she? When will I meet her?" Sam wondered if he'd somehow missed this information.

"You'll find out soon. So start tonight, Sam. Prioritizing is not an easy assignment. Many people fail at this point. I pray you won't."

"Okay," Sam said, obviously still confused. He fumbled with the leather pieces in front of him and stacked them neatly, tidying up before he left.

"Sam, while you meditate on these two foundation laws, please help me finish stitching these shoes. The customers tomorrow will need comfortable footwear while they cook dinner, read to their children, clean their chimneys, wash clothes, or maybe attend to a sick spouse. Yes, it's very important that we finish!"

And so they did.

8

Facing the Truth

The children were put to bed, the dishes had been cleared and washed, the curtains were drawn, and the fire was stoked. Sam and Suzette sat before the hearth quietly holding hands while waiting for the other to begin.

"I think…" Sam finally said.

"We can…" Suzette said at the same time.

The two laughed softly.

"You think what, Sam?" Suzette asked.

"We can what, Suzette?" Sam asked at the same time.

They laughed a bit more as light from the fire flickered on the walls.

"I think we should pray first," Suzette suggested.

"We can begin with prayer," Sam said at the same time.

They looked at each other, laughing even more and smiling.

"Okay, why don't we pray silently, and then we can pray together aloud," Sam said.

So they both bowed their heads and prayed, their hearts open to God's compassion, love, strength, and leadership. They praised God for being willing to lead them to true fulfillment, trust, and openness to life and love. Peace permeated the room as they communed with God and asked Him to lead them and help them know and live His ways.

Then they took turns praying aloud, giving thanks to the Creator who held them in His arms, asking for guidance and grace, and acknowledging that the best life is filled with His truth, promise, hope, and love, and this can only be realized fully through an intimate relationship with Him and by living within His divine plan.

After saying amen, Sam and Suzette looked into each other's eyes a bit self-consciously but full of love for each other and hope for their future. Then they began the difficult discussion, bringing up the subjects they'd avoided for so long. They talked about being over their heads financially, and worse, that negativity and frustration was eating away at the fabric of their love and home.

Sam admitted he was the primary cause of their financial problems. Suzette assured him that they were in this together. Back and forth the conversation went as they explored where they were and how they got there. Then Suzette said, "Sam, let's stop recounting the errors. You need to stop blaming and punishing yourself, stop making me the 'long-suffering wife,' and stop searching for the way out."

Sam blinked. "But we must find a way out! And with God's help—"

"We *are* out, Sam. With God's help we are already out. Yes, we need to honor our financial commitments and change our outlooks, but that doesn't mean we're stuck where we were. Do you see that? We *are* out. We're here, together, with God. From here we move forward with new resolve to handle things differently and renewed hearts filled with God's love and love for each other. We have so much already, Sam. We are truly blessed."

Sam hugged Suzette. "My dear love, you are beautiful. You are precious. And you are right. How could I forget Magowin's first lesson? He taught me that no one can live a rich life until he knows he is rich already. We *do* have much to be thankful for, Suzette, and today we begin a new path."

"It won't be easy."

"No, it won't," Sam agreed. "But we'll be all right and make it through."

"So we'll begin now, okay? We'll start not by listing our debts but by listing our joys, blessings, and values," Suzette suggested.

"Listing? Yes! When I first met with Magowin, he sent me home to think about…" Sam paused and grabbed his wife's hands. "Suzette, he asked me to think about so many questions that they whirled in my head. I don't know if I can remember them all, but he asked me today to go over them with you during this…this discussion."

Suzette smiled. She knew how Sam disliked discussions. And she knew how she loved this man despite watching him slide into misery during the last few years. Through Sam's ups and downs, she'd maintained her small sewing business and taught the children their lessons. God had helped her keep her heart and mind on Him and her work for Him as a wife, mother, businesswoman, and community member. And though this had sustained her, she'd known the day would come when Sam's sliding foundation would crumble. But she'd also known that there was a strong foundation they would rediscover together, a solid base strong enough to build on. Still smiling, Suzette asked, "And those questions?"

Sam settled back in his chair. "Okay, if I can remember… And Magowin said we're to go over them so that we can consider how God wants us to prioritize them."

"That's great. The first question?"

"Well, Magowin asked, 'Who are you really, Sam? Why do you want to be prosperous?'"

Suzette laughed. "Surely that wasn't the very first question!"

"Well, that was one of the last ones. But the first ones were extreme. He asked that I review my *entire* life. And to consider how I was raised to view money and wealth. You know, how my family made a living, and what they and the villagers taught me about finances. He said to review my beliefs about saving and giving and spending. I was also to think about what I enjoyed about my work and what I think about at work. It was so much, Suzette. Do you remember that I stayed up all night trying to think about what I was supposed to think about? And he also asked me how much I include you in financial decisions. And why I was attracted to you in the first place."

"I like that one!" Suzette exclaimed. "Do you know why I was attracted to you?" Suzette glanced sideways at Sam.

"I believe I charmed you," Sam said, returning her gaze.

"My dear husband, I fell in love with you because I saw a noble, searching soul. I saw a man who loved his work and was kind to his fellow workers. I saw a man who stopped to help strangers and who took the time to study the craftsmanship of more experienced tradesmen. And I saw a man who looked at me with true love in his eyes. I suppose you did charm me a bit. But I'm more pragmatic than that, Sam. I saw God working through your heart, and this was by far the best quality that drew me to you. I felt that God had brought you into my life. I still feel that way."

Sam looked down. "Suzette, I don't know what to say. Surely I have disappointed you."

"Do you love God? Do you love me and the children?"

"Of course! With all my heart."

"Then I can never be disappointed. Yes, life hasn't always been smooth, but my love for you hasn't changed. Now, it's your turn. What attracted you to me the first time?"

"I was attracted to you because I thought—and still think—you are incredibly special. You are wise, patient, talented, and radiant.

I could think of no greater blessing in my life than to have such a special woman share her life with me. You are simply beautiful. I love you so much, And I want to share everything with you."

"Even your financial decisions? Even your money and borrowing decisions?"

Sam looked down again. "Yes, that is difficult for me. I haven't included you very much. I think..."

"Don't think, Sam. Talk. Let's tackle Magowin's questions. Let's begin with our financial backgrounds. I'll go first to help you ease into it."

It was a long discussion as they moved from a woman raised comfortably as the daughter of shepherds who lived in a small home on the grounds of a large manor house to a man raised as a wood gatherer in rather poor conditions, and how Sam dreamed of finding or doing something more with his life. They talked about how Sam never learned to read but could calculate figures and devise new tools. They talked about how Suzette was tutored in the manor house by the gracious mistress.

Their discussion lasted well into the evening. Sam rose several times to add wood to the fire, especially when the discussion became awkward or hinted at becoming heated. He wanted the finest things for the children, but Suzette wanted their children to lead fine lives. Sam was nervous about what people would think if they gave up their large home for something more modest. Suzette cared what God thought, not what the townsfolk might think.

They discussed the children's lessons—what they wanted to teach them about money, life, and spiritual matters. They discussed each other's spending habits, saving habits (or lack thereof), and when to include the other person in a variety of financial decisions.

All these things can be difficult subjects for anyone with a human nature, but discuss they did. And time after time they returned to God and prayer, asking Him to guide them.

"Loving God and following His principles and teachings are our top priority, Suzette. I know this, though at times I'm afraid to simply follow what my heart tells me is right. I do recapture that amazing certainty of God's love and direction during times of prayer and reflection, like I did the other day in the forest when I was gathering wood. Yes, God must be the first priority. From that base, we can prioritize everything else. This is what Magowin said, and I know it to be true. Do you agree?"

Suzette nodded.

They both sat back and took a long, restful moment quietly staring at the fire. Taking a deep breath, Sam asked, "Suzette, are you ready to continue?"

With a nod, Suzette leaned forward, and they tackled prioritizing other aspects of their lives. They covered the spiritual needs of the entire family, the children specifically, and then what they needed as a couple and as individuals.

They discussed which forms of misbehavior from the children warranted what degree of discipline. They decided to make love and praise a priority over pointing out faults.

Then they moved on to how to respond to mishaps and crises, which almost naturally lead to the most pressing crisis from Sam's point of view—finances, especially the mortgage, the bills, and the financial pressure he put himself under.

"I feel that earning enough to pay the bills should be a high priority for me. This will help you, the children, and me."

"If you earn enough to maintain a high lifestyle, that's wonderful, Sam. But if you don't and we have to cut back, will you feel like you've failed? Wouldn't a better priority be to work diligently so as to earn an honest income? And then we will adjust what we spend according to that income so we live below our means. That way we can also put some money aside for savings."

"But the house…" Sam looked around. "Having a roof over our

heads is important, and this house let's people know I'm a good contractor. But it's a struggle to make the payments, especially now that business has slowed way down."

"We can sell this house or turn it over to Geoffrey the moneylender."

"No! I can't do that. I—"

"Remember our priorities, Sam. This house is nice, but it's not what makes us a family. And it is more than we need. Our family won't be happy if you are so stressed out and focused on earning more and more so we can afford the payments. Tell me, Sam, what *is* your goal in life?" Suzette playfully nudged Sam.

Sam visibly relaxed and asked with some amusement, "You mean, 'Who are you really, Sam? Why do you want to be prosperous?'"

Suzette laughed before responding, "I guess so."

"I want to be successful in a building business. I want it so much it almost hurts. I love the feel of wood and stone in my hands. I enjoy designing and crafting a new house or building. And experiencing the camaraderie of a fine crew is wonderful. I know I've lost my zeal for meeting…no for going beyond…the customers' needs and wants. And the best men on my crew took jobs with other foremen. And even the ones I have now aren't very pleased to be working with me. I find this extremely painful in my heart.

"Who am I? I'm a simple wood gatherer, I suppose, who dreamed of creating a better life. And after I met you and we had children, I wanted something better for the people I love. I'm a man who now faces uncertainty. Tomorrow I begin the last contract on the books. I have to face the truth that I've not succeeded in earning a living at what I love to do. Or at least what I used to love to do." He looked away from his wife, ashamed of what he'd just admitted for the first time.

"Sam, please don't—"

"Suzette," Sam cut in, "we *did* need to have this discussion. I do want to trust God more, and I know I need to confer with you more before making decisions. I know I've made some rather rash financial investments, and some of my choices haven't been good. I admit that. But this information doesn't tell me what I should do right now to meet our obligations. And the next mortgage payment is due in three short weeks!"

"In three weeks your current project will be completed—or nearly completed," offered Suzette. "Concentrate on your building. When the mortgage due date arrives, we'll figure out what to do. For now, I encourage you to just love your work. Feel blessed by it, do your best by it, and support the people who work for you."

"You make it sound so simple, but it's not. How can I not worry about keeping this roof over our heads?"

"You have made your life—our lives—too complicated. Your focus is on prestige and making more…and more, and more money. With that as your motive, I'm sure my suggestions sound too simple."

The words stung, and Sam remained silent.

"Sam, I know correcting our situation isn't going to be simple." Suzette paused, and quiet filled the room. Finally she said, "Why do we discipline and teach the children?"

"Isn't that obvious?" Sam asked. "We do it because we're their parents."

"I believe the answer is even more simple. If we did it just because we're their parents, that would mean it was merely a duty—and duty can only motivate for so long. Duty isn't our core motive. Think about it again, Sam. Why do we put so much effort into showing them the best way? There is a much simpler answer."

Sam stared into the fire and then looked at his patient wife. "Because we want to. Because we love them."

"We love them," echoed Suzette. "That's our true motivating force. Our love for God, for life, and for each other flows into our love for them. Not just because they are our blood and in our care, but because they are children—ours and God's—and we can't help but love them unconditionally. We so naturally act on that love that we sometimes don't even think about love as our primary motive."

"You're right. Of course that's right. We aren't primarily motivated by duty but by abiding love. But what has this to do with work and finances?"

Suzette kissed Sam's cheek. "I believe it has everything to do with everything!"

Sam looked at Suzette. Her eyes were dancing, and she appeared radiant. "Suzette," he marveled, "you're aglow. What do you have that makes you sparkle like that?"

"Do you know why I work, Sam? Do you know why I look forward to receiving sewing commissions?"

"Because you love sewing and crafting fine clothing and linens. And because you do it so well and are rewarded for your work."

"That is part of it. Yes, it's what I do well, and God has gifted me with these talents. And He asked me to use them for His work. He has also asked me to love, so I use my work to love others."

Suzette paused and they both stared into the fire for a minute or two. Sam seemed to be pondering what his wife had shared. Suzette looked at Sam and smiled before continuing.

"Sam, I truly love my customers—even the grouchy ones. When I sew a buttonhole, I imagine that man or woman preparing for the day. I love that person and pray for them. So I put love into that buttonhole. When I stitch a flower into a baby coverlet, I love that child yet to be born. So I entwine love into that stitching. Do my customers know? I'm not sure. But I'm not motivated by whether or not they know I love them or that I show my love through my work for them. I'm thankful God blesses me for loving others. I've never wanted for customers or work, so I hope my love does shine through my work. Love inspires and motivates me to work. God allows me to minister to people through my skills, and I'm blessed with joy and monetary payment."

After a moment of silence, Sam said, "And I know, dear wife, that you're going to tell me how this relates to me."

"Sam, you must not simply love your work or the monetary rewards of work. That is misplaced love and motive. If money is your motive, you won't find true, lasting happiness. For people who focus on money, there is never enough of it. Instead, focus on loving God through your work. Set your priorities according to His wisdom. Love and serve people in His name in a way that utilizes your talents and skills. The true motive is love. Real, unconditional, God-centered love."

"Are you saying I need to love the people who have asked me to build their houses or buildings?"

"Yes. It's that simple, Sam. Forget the money and concentrate on loving your customers and those who will live or work in the building. You also need to love your workers and what God allows you to create together in His name."

"Hmmm. The folks I'm building the next house for aren't particularly pleasant. In fact, they're somewhat surly. I'm the only one in this area who agreed to take on their project. They can be mean-spirited, and I'm fairly sure they'll complain at every step."

"Just concentrate on loving them through your work. God doesn't ask us to love just sweet people or those who need love. All people need to experience love. And I know God gives us the courage and strength to love even the unlovable. Search your heart, Sam. God has given you the desire to love. Choose to be motivated by love in all you do. I know you too well to not be sure love is in your heart. I believe you're afraid that if you let love be your primary motive it will interfere with profits."

As Sam took in the truth and wisdom reflected in Suzette's

words, he realized he needed time to take it all in. "I must think on what you've said," he finally said.

"That's great, Sam. It's time to go to sleep anyway. We're both weary from this important discussion. I love you, Sam. And I'll pray for peace and wisdom for you. In a few short hours you will begin work on the house for those cranky customers who need your love."

They both laughed, and the residual tension dissolved. They ended their late evening with humor and hopeful hearts.

And the next day...

Sam rose early for his early morning time with the Lord. After reading from the Bible and praising God, Sam prayed, "Thank You, Lord, for the truth You shared through Suzette last night. Please give me the courage to show Your love through my work, and give me the wisdom to share this new approach with my crew. I love You. Amen."

After dressing for work, Sam ate breakfast. He kissed Suzette goodbye and went to work with joy in his heart.

He met his crew at dawn at the cleared site. The men stood beside stacks of lumber and stone, awaiting Sam's orders. But Sam just stood there and looked at them. Then he looked at his shoes. He looked up and his gaze wandered to some distant trees. Finally he turned to the crew.

"Men, I need to ask your forgiveness. For some time now I've focused on making money instead of serving our customers by doing quality work and adding the special touches that make our projects outstanding. With God's help, I've discovered my priorities were wrong. So now, with your help, I want to focus on giving our customers the best house we can build. Today we're more than laborers; we're also dream makers. We need to work within our budget, yes, but I encourage you to do your best work even if it takes a bit more time. And if you think of extra features we can easily add to the project for minimal cost, let's discuss it. I want us to be proud of what we accomplish and have customers who are well pleased with our work."

At first the men were stunned. They stared at him, expecting that any moment his usual scowl would appear and he would start barking orders like he'd done every morning on this job.

Sam went on. "Men, today we're going to add something to our building materials that I've been leaving out for too long. Today we're adding something more permanent than mortar, more enduring than stone, and more valuable than fine wood. Today we're going to add love."

The crewmen glanced at each other and then back at Sam, revealing their uncertainty about how to respond to this new approach. They remained silent, fidgeting uneasily. *What's wrong with the boss?* was their unspoken question. Most seemed uncomfortable, and some were frowning in irritation. In the back row, one man leaned close to a coworker and said, "I'd heard he was having money problems. Has it finally driven him over the edge?" Their confusion was broken by Sam's firm voice.

"Thomas!"

The crew snapped to attention.

"Thomas, you will lead the crew today in making forms and laying stones for the foundation. I want each stone to be set meticulously, taking great care to make sure the layers stay level. And, Thomas, we're not going to use substandard timber for the flooring as we've done in the past. Instead, we'll use the best wood available. Do you know why?"

"Because the owners of the house asked for this?"

"No, Thomas. Because we should always do our best and take pride in our work. These people, their children, and someday their grandchildren will walk and play on these floors. Because we love and care for them, we want the floors to be sturdy and pleasing to the eye. We want the owners to have peace of mind that the floors will wear well and resist rotting. We want the floors to reflect that we care about the project, but even more, that we care about the people we're building for. As we construct the stone foundation today, let's think about this new approach. Let's remember that this foundation is going to support a fine floor for people we care about. Let's work!"

And so they did. As they constructed the foundation on the neatly graded dirt, the men whispered among themselves that Sam obviously wasn't quite himself. And though it took some getting used to, they were intrigued by Sam's new attitude. Gradually they rediscovered the pride and satisfaction that came with working hard and doing their best. By lunch break, the crew welcomed Sam's new tone. By the middle of the afternoon, some were whistling while they worked. And by the end of the day, a sturdy, well-crafted, level foundation was finished.

"Thank you, men," Sam said. "Together we have done a good job today. I'm blessed to have you on my crew. I'll see you tomorrow morning. Have a good evening."

That night Sam recounted his day. "Suzette, I applied your words of wisdom at work today. I think the men found it a bit puzzling and maybe even a bit amusing. From now on, I intend to stress that building this house is a labor of love for the people who will make it their home. And at the end..."

"At the end, Sam, we'll see what money we have and visit the moneylender. For now, that's the best course, is it not? So let's sit down and enjoy this soup and bread I've prepared." Then Suzette's eyes twinkled as she added, "I prepared this meal with love because I knew you would be eating it!"

The next morning, and every day on the job after that, Sam reminded the crew at every step to be thinking about the people who would be enjoying their new house. When the owners came for inspections, they sometimes criticized and found faults, which sorely tested Sam's resolve. But Sam reiterated to his crew that they were not to think on the unhappiness shown by these folks, but rather to focus on the happiness the owners might experience by living in such a well-built place.

The more he expressed this motivation, the more he felt alive within. The more he talked of the importance of each detail, the more peace he felt with the work. The more he concentrated on the giving and loving aspects of the work, the more joy and fulfillment filled his heart. And by the quality of their work, Sam was sure his crewmen were experiencing the same thing.

Every window was crafted with love for the people who would open its shutters to greet the day. The hearth was carefully designed and constructed to exude warmth even when a fire wasn't present. The doors were smoothly planed and sanded to be lovely to the touch. Ledges were added to walls to hold flower vases and family mementos. The roof was pitched more steeply than Sam had recently designed. This construction was more difficult for Sam and the roofers, but Sam knew that steep roofs could withstand the rain, sleet, and snow that often caused "usual fare" roofs to leak, crack, and cave in.

Each evening Sam told Suzette of the progress, and each evening Suzette welcomed home a man who had a lighter step and seemed to have a lighter heart. Sam was a man who served God by loving the work and customers God blessed him with.

The house was nearly complete, and the mortgage due date was fast approaching. Sam knew he needed to set up an appointment to talk about his own mortgage with Geoffrey. He went to see him after work one Friday. When Geoffrey answered the door, Sam asked to make an appointment to discuss the mortgage, preferably next week when the next payment was due.

"That will be suitable. Next Friday, anytime after the midday meal, I'll be here."

"Next Friday in the afternoon it is. My wife will be coming too."

"Certainly," responded Geoffrey with his usual soft tone of voice. "I think that is most wise."

"Thank you. We'll come next week." Sam shook Geoffrey's hand and turned to leave. He was amazed at how relaxed he felt. He was buoyed by the success he felt with this house, and he hadn't thought about the profit from it—or rather, he hadn't been distracted with thoughts of profit. He was feeling so calm that when he passed Magowin's little cobbler shop, he paused and then went in.

"Sam!" Magowin's face broke into a wide, jubilant grin as he came forward to usher his student and friend into his shop.

"I see you're making black leather boots, Magowin. Very fancy."

"Ho ho, my friend! They are for the duchess and her daughters. They are avid horsewomen, you know. You look well, my young student!"

"Ah, Magowin, you warm my heart. I miss you. But I have been very, very busy with a house…"

"I know of this new house. It is four streets over. There is good talk of this house. Very good talk. It is said that the crew is in love with this house, and that everyone is envious of the future owners. They are getting more than they bargained for, eh?" Magowin's eyes were twinkling.

Sam laughed. "I suppose you're right. But this house has helped me come out of a mournful state, so I don't regret a small loss of profit. This house has been a blessing, for I know now what is truly most enjoyable about my labor. To be of service and to work with love and an honorable spirit."

"Your wheels have certainly been set in motion," marveled Magowin. "I fear I have no hope of your giving up on the building trade to join me in the footwear business."

"One never knows," Sam said. He laughed. "I have no prospects as yet for my next project. But I'm feeling more motivated now than I've felt in years. I'm very hopeful that I can help with another project soon."

"And what motivates you, Sam?" Magowin eyed him keenly.

"This may sound rather simple, but love motivates me. I want to express my love for God by loving people the way I used to. I want to offer them my services and my talents, and I want to work knowing that I am contributing to their lives in some way. I want to see my business not just as a source of income, but as a way to express my love for God, life, and people."

"You want to build with God at your side."

"Yes, Magowin. I have not forgotten the Laws of Wisdom and Priority. They have led me to this new outlook. Actually, Suzette, my wise and persistent wife, reminded me of what my focus should be. She is an amazing woman, Magowin."

"Yes, and an amazing teacher! Did I not say that your next teacher would be an expert on the third law?"

"The third law? What do you mean? Suzette? How…?"

"The third law is the *Law of Motive*. Until you acknowledge with your heart and soul that meaningful living and work are motivated by loving God and, through Him, loving others, you can't achieve true, lasting prosperity."

Awe flooded through Sam. "How did you know my wife would lead me to this?" he whispered.

"Because I know her work. I see the care she puts into it, which reflects her love for God and, through Him, her love for people. I see love in her eyes as she hands me the clothes I purchase. Never once—never, Sam—has she skimped on those clothes, even though she does not charge me full price for them. Every article is stitched to withstand a hundred washings. The embroidery is flawless. You should see the mothers who receive Suzette's dresses and bed linens and curtains. Their eyes are filled with gratitude. The women are overwhelmed by the obvious love that has gone into each piece. And you ask how I knew that Suzette would teach you about the blessing of putting love into work?" Magowin slapped Sam on the back. "My very wonderful man, how could I *not* know? All that was needed was for your heart and ears to be open!"

"Does this mean I'm to learn the fourth law soon? Am I to rejoin you in your shop after all?"

"No fear, Sam! You will be building again soon. I have faith in this. No, you must visit Geoffrey to learn the fourth law."

"Geoffrey! How strange that you should say this! I have an appointment with him in one week regarding my debt."

"Hmm, regarding what you owe. Yes, he'll undertake that matter with you, of course. But he will also teach you something about freedom."

"Freedom? Magowin, you puzzle me, but I have learned to trust you."

Magowin smiled warmly into Sam's trusting eyes. "I am so happy to hear this, Sam, because I craft my words with love, knowing they will fall not only upon your ears but also into your heart."

9
A Generous Spirit

Sam and his loyal crew attracted attention during the construction of the house "built with love." Every day many townspeople strolled by to watch the progress and listen to the cheery camaraderie of the men who seemed to take such pride in this one house.

And they asked questions. "Why is the path to the door not straight, but elegantly curved?"

"Because there is to be a planting of flowers beneath this tree, and we thought it would be nice for the owners to walk past that spot as they come home each day," was the reply.

"Why is there a ramp built up to the back stoop?"

"So that water buckets can be brought into the house by cart. Won't that be more convenient for the owners?"

The townspeople marveled that the crew cared about the comfort of the owners. Their craftsmanship was superb, and their singing and whistling in jovial harmony was uplifting. To be sure, a stop to see "the house" had become a must every day even for the busiest tradespeople and for harried mothers with children in tow.

The day before his scheduled meeting with Geoffrey, Sam received the third of four installment payments on the project. The tax collector showed up at the site to collect the king's share.

He took time to admire this cozy house that seemed to have its own warm spirit.

The tax collector felt uncomfortable hanging about. He was not a well-received official. But this house looked so inviting. It was just the kind he would love to have for his wife and new baby boy. Catching Sam's attention and pulling him aside, he hesitantly asked Sam when he would be available to build a nice cottage for his family.

"My good man," replied Sam, "I am not as busy as you might suppose. I can begin in about one week's time, when this project is finished."

"So soon!" The tax collector 's heart was joyous. "Truly? I will draw up the papers! My wife will be very happy. I have not dared to ask anyone to build a house for me. I feared no one would be willing or they might try to cheat me because of my job. It's not easy being a tax collector for the king."

Sam clapped the tax collector on the back. "My team would be honored to build a house for your family. And we will give you only our best work." Then with a chuckle he added, "What better way to again see some of those coins that I have handed over to you today, yes?"

That evening, Sam and Suzette readied for their meeting with the loan agent. The mortgage payment was eight hundred royal coins and, after Sam's crew had been paid their share, they still had twelve hundred. They were relieved that they held enough for tomorrow, but wished they had enough to cover the next month's expenses and the next mortgage payment. With no firm contracts in hand and only one prospect, Sam finally admitted that they should probably not keep their house. Yet this didn't upset him like he thought it would.

The next day at noon, Sam and Suzette cheerfully took the

children to the neighbor's house, and then they went to Geoffrey's with quiet resolve.

"Come in, please," Geoffrey said at their knock. "I've prepared some tea for us." Geoffrey ushered them in.

A person has to listen intently to catch all Geoffrey's words because they were few and always spoken softly, Sam thought. Once seated, Sam spoke up. "Geoffrey, I'll get right to the point. We've brought the payment for this month, but I can't guarantee we will have next month's payment. I have eight hundred coins for you." Sam placed a strong cloth pouch before Geoffrey. "I have four hundred still in my purse. I will receive one more payment in a week, when my project is complete, which will indeed give me the next payment, but as you know, there will be food to buy and expenses for this coming month. Suzette will have earnings from her business, and I do have someone interested in having a house built, but at this time I have no contract in hand."

Sam took a breath. "So, Geoffrey, we are in need of your... well, your advice as to how to proceed. Should we pay extra interest and put off paying for a few months until I'm back on my feet? Should we sell the house and move into a cozier one? Should we turn this house back to you and move? We're at a loss as to how to handle this obligation." Sam looked at his hands, then at Suzette, then to Geoffrey.

Geoffrey looked gently at the two before him. "And so..." he began. Sam and Suzette leaned forward to hear him clearly. "So you will have at least six hundred forty coins for the upcoming month. Will this get you through?" He looked at Suzette.

"Six hundred forty? Well, that would not be enough to live on, I'm afraid, but actually we'll have eight hundred from Sam's pay and—"

Geoffrey put up his hand slowly and looked back at Sam. "You will have next month's mortgage, Sam. Take comfort in that. But perhaps you are correct. I think this house of yours is too much for your means…and needs."

Sam and Suzette were confused. Had they heard Geoffrey clearly? What was this six hundred forty figure he was using? And how could he know that Sam would have next month's mortgage?

Sam spoke. "I have foolishly obligated us to a house that is too costly, and I am ashamed to have borrowed what I cannot easily repay. But what did you just say about six hundred forty coins?"

"Marcus the tax collector came in last evening to see me about a loan for a house that he said you will build for him. I'm sure you will build a fine house for this man. You will be blessed to serve him. And I, I will have the opportunity to serve him in ways he doesn't yet realize."

Geoffrey's voice was so quiet that Sam and Suzette almost felt as if they were listening to someone praying.

"Yes, you will have next month's mortgage, Sam and Suzette. But this is not my main concern." Again he looked at Suzette. "Six hundred forty coins will not see you through?"

Suzette puzzled over how to respond. "I will have enough. As we said, Sam will have eight hundred coins by next week, and I will earn four hundred fifty coins from my sewing. Of course, fifty will go toward taxes, but this leaves twelve hundred for the monthly expenses. That will be sufficient. But why do you want to know about my expenses?"

"My dear Suzette, I care greatly about your financial health. I have no wish for any loan you may have with me to disrupt your happiness or harmony. I wish for you and Sam true prosperity. Tell me, can you get by on a thousand coins for the month?"

"A thousand? That would be difficult, but we'll have twelve hundred, Geoffrey—"

Again Geoffrey put up his hand. He smiled warmly at the two.

"You have described earnings of two thousand royal coins to me, yes? Twelve hundred so far on Sam's project, four hundred more to come, and Suzette's four hundred."

"Yes, that's right," replied Sam. "We've paid the taxes already, and we're paying eight hundred to you. So that leaves us twelve hundred for the month."

"What will you pay God?"

Sam and Suzette were silent, taken aback. Hesitantly, Suzette said, "We are not selfish people, Geoffrey. Truly not. Each month I sell articles at reduced prices for the poor. It is a joy to do so. And we give money to the church when we can."

"That's fine. That is indeed fine. And I am not here to judge you. It is because I love you and I know you are seeking God's ways that I bring this up. Listen with your heart. Until you give away the first fruits of what you earn to God's service and those in need, which is called a 'tithe,' you will not fully appreciate and enjoy your wealth. The traditional amount to give is ten percent. Based on that, giving on an income of two thousand coins would be two hundred coins. That is a good tithe amount. I give well beyond that, and I encourage you to consider doing so as well."

Sam, whose heart had opened so much since his meetings with Magowin began, suddenly felt cornered and overwhelmed again.

"Geoffrey, you are obviously a man who speaks of what is right. We came to you with great anticipation today, especially me, for Magowin the cobbler said you would speak to me of freedom. But right now I feel more burdened. We are not ready to set aside an additional ten percent of our earnings for the needy. I have committed myself to serving God. We have committed ourselves." Sam took Suzette's hand. "We have opened our minds to His wisdom and guidance. I have discovered new peace and joy in loving and serving others through my work. At this time, is this not enough? Must I also give away the precious coins my family needs?"

"You do indeed have generous spirits." Geoffrey placed his hands on their clasped hands. "You are blessed. I see this in the house you are building, Sam. I see this in the dresses my wife purchases from you, Suzette. You are walking an honest path. But if you are seeking complete freedom—including financial freedom—you must release yourself to giving in all ways with all your sources of energy. This includes your money."

Geoffrey reached out and refilled everyone's tea. "Tell me, Sam. If you were a very wealthy man, would you enjoy giving your money to God and for helping others?"

Sam's face brightened. "Oh yes! Very much!"

"I see your eyes light up—that would be…well, fun, wouldn't it?"

"It would be wonderful to be so generous and benevolent. This would be a good dream to have."

"Why are you denying yourself this dream?"

Sam was speechless.

Geoffrey continued. "Suzette, do Sam's eyes light up like this when he has his horse carts serviced?"

Suzette was relieved to laugh and ease the tension. "No, I should say not."

"Yet he chooses to own two carts that he gets no pleasure in the financial burden of their upkeep." Geoffrey turned back to Sam. "Does the extra cart give you as much joy as the joy you felt when you thought about benevolent giving?"

"I…well, I suppose not, but…"

"Yes?"

"I'm not a wealthy man yet." Suddenly Sam heard his own words and took in a breath. "No, that is not true. I *am* a wealthy man. I am following the laws Magowin has revealed to me, and the first step was to see how blessed and prosperous I am as a creation of God. I *am* wealthy in many ways, Geoffrey. But not with money...at least not at this point."

"But you are on the path to prosperity?"

"Yes!"

"You wish to succeed and prosper in life? You wish to lead a significant life?"

"With all my heart."

"Then you must experience an even deeper partnership with God by giving back a portion of what you earn to God's work and to others whom the Creator also loves and cares for."

"But, Geoffrey, I don't know that I can afford to make my required payments to you if I must also give ten percent away."

"Sam, if you can't afford to give, then you are indeed living beyond your means. And you are depriving yourself of great happiness."

Again Sam was silent.

Suzette turned to her husband. "He's right, Sam. We're not getting great joy from our possessions. Some we truly do need, but most are simply things we wanted. And I've noticed the pleasure from owning things wears off quickly. I'm feeling at peace about this conversation. I would rather live more modestly and share what we have than live in dread of the bills coming in. I know we can do this, Sam. I know we can be more generous with our God-given time, talents, money, and the other resources. What a great way to honor Jesus and point people to Him. And just think how much this would teach our daughters about how generous God is with His gifts and what He wants us to do with them."

Sam looked away and stared at a corner of the room. "This is not what I expected to hear today. I came to discuss paying my debt, and I learn that I am to keep even less of my money to live on." He turned back to the two who sat with him. He saw the understanding and care in their eyes. "We will do this, Suzette and I. This is the right thing to do."

Geoffrey nodded. "I am speaking to you not as a loan agent. Rather, I'm coming to you with this truth as a fellow believer in the one true God. I saw our meeting as an opportunity to speak to your heart and to Suzette's heart. You will reach your dreams, Sam and Suzette, by following this fourth rule to give a tithe to God and to share with people less fortunate. The fourth law is about sharing your wealth."

"Yes, I figured this was the next law," Sam said, looking into Geoffrey's eyes.

Geoffrey smiled. "The *Law of Generosity* is not merely a duty or a commandment. This law is a means to increase your happiness and even your wealth. You're asked to accept even more that you are an instrument and even a partner of God. You see, Sam and Suzette, *God does not send abundance into our lives so we can live lavishly. No, it's so we can generously share with others His generosity to us.* As you help others, you help those whom God also cherishes. He wants to work with you, Sam and Suzette. He wants to give you the opportunity to help and participate in His blessings. He desires your heart, your prayers, your devotion, your joys, and your wealth in all its forms."

Sam and Suzette looked at each other. Sam said, "This is a lot to take in, but we will discuss it and put it into practice. This fourth law sounds difficult, but I'm sure it brings great blessings."

"That's great, Sam. And we'll discuss your next house payment next month. Today, take two hundred coins from the four hundred you have in your pocket and take them to the pastor of your church."

Although Sam and Suzette wondered how they would make it until their next paycheck, they agreed to follow Geoffrey's suggestion.

"Trust God's ways, Sam and Suzette. Today you will feel great satisfaction and more freedom. Have faith in your heart's dream to be a giver. When you come back in a month, you can tell me about your newfound freedom!"

With very few words, Sam and Suzette thanked Geoffrey, counted out two hundred coins from their purse, secured them in a little pouch Geoffrey graciously provided, and then took their leave. They proceeded to the small chapel they attended just down the road from the moneylender's office. When they arrived, they looked at each other, smiled, nodded, withdrew the pouch, and then Sam knocked on the wooden door of the pastor's cottage next to the church.

The pastor was a young, enthusiastic man who had lived in the town just a few short years. Already, however, he was beloved. He worked tirelessly to minister to his congregants and the other people in the town. After he opened his door, he greeted Sam and Suzette joyfully. "What a blessed surprise! Suzette, I was just mentioning your name. I'm hoping to start a school for the children in town. So few can read, you know, and it has always been my dream to share the sacred literature with as many as possible. If I could start a school in my home, what a great blessing this would be to the children. And I hope to include any adults who wish to learn too. I know, Suzette, that you read and that you teach your children. I was just mentioning your name in prayer, hoping you might consider helping." Pastor Wright's eyes twinkled as he glanced at Sam and then looked at Suzette again.

Suzette nodded and laughed. "If you need my help, Pastor Wright, I will certainly contribute. I would be honored to be a teacher. Even my oldest child can help instruct the youngest students."

"Praise God!" exclaimed the young pastor. And with a comical look toward the sky he added, "And now, Father, if You could arrange for the schoolbooks to knock upon my door, I will be even more grateful and truly amazed!"

"Perhaps you can buy them with this," Sam said as he handed the small pouch to the pastor. "It is but two hundred royal coins, but perhaps it will help."

The normally exuberant man fell silent. He looked at the pouch in his hand with tears running down his face.

"Surely they will buy enough supplies to get the school started," Suzette said, breaking the awkward silence.

Pastor Wright looked up and smiled broadly. "It will, indeed. I thank you! And God thanks you. Your generosity is perfectly timed. God works in astounding ways!"

"You are more than welcome," said Suzette. "I will call on you tomorrow to help plan your school."

And the next day...

Suzette was preparing the evening meal when Sam came through the door. "Where have you been this fine Saturday afternoon with no word to your wife?" she chided him good-naturedly.

"I sold one of my horse carts to Thomas. He's been saving for a long time, and I knew my used one would be less expensive than a new one for him. It's in great shape and will work just fine for what he needs." Sam placed a bag of coins on the table. "Three hundred royal coins. Two hundred are for your household expenses, and if you agree, you can take the other hundred to Pastor Wright's on Monday for the church or the school."

"Sam, you always said that only a poor man had one cart only. You won't miss this cart?" Suzette asked.

"I will never miss that cart. And now there are two things I will possess forever."

Suzette beamed with pride at her husband. She hugged him, kissed him, and then asked, "And what are the two things?"

"For as long as I live, I will have the memory of Thomas's overjoyed face when I offered him a very good bargain on my fine cart. And I will treasure the look on Pastor Wright's face when we handed him those coins yesterday as part of our offering to God. Being generous has strengthened my faith and brought much satisfaction. Life is so exciting now, Suzette. Now, I'm famished. What's for supper?"

10
A Deeper Understanding

Sam and his crew stood a while admiring their work. The house wasn't particularly large, but it was solidly built and seemed to welcome its owners, visitors, and passersby. The stonework was precise, the timber framing was attractive and functional, the window ledges were generous (enough for two pies or several flowerpots), and even the modest patch of earth that led to the doorway was thoughtfully prepared, complete with paving, rock terracing, and flowering plants. A comfortable bench sat beneath a small oak in front of the house.

This was construction to the highest standards. This house was one the new owners could be proud of. And this was a house that would last for several generations, and each generation would know by the details and quality that this place was built with gifted hands and caring hearts.

Sam's heart was swelling that day. Not only had his crew finished a very successful project together, but he had received news from Grecco that several more folks had inquired into hiring Sam's crew to build a stable, a shop, another house, and even do some repair work on several bridges in the area.

The slight chill in the air was barely noticeable as Sam glowed with contentment. Silently he praised God for this beautiful day and for leading him to this new path. He asked Him to bless Suzette for believing in him, Magowin for redirecting him, and Geoffrey for his patient teaching. *How exciting it will be to tell Geoffrey that making the mortgage payment isn't going to be a problem anymore,* Sam thought. Yes, life was definitely back on track.

The new owners paid Sam the last installment and, despite their negative reputation, expressed great pleasure in their new place. Sam humbly responded, "My crew and I thank you for the opportunity to serve and build for you. We have enjoyed this work. May you and your family always find happiness here."

Sam paid each crewman and then paid Marcus the taxman, who was especially happy to see this project completed because his was next on Sam's docket.

"I've partially cleared my land, Sam. I can't tell you how excited my wife and I are to have our own house built at last. Not that we haven't appreciated the king's generous lodgings within the castle's walls. My wife is a gardener, you see, and I've always wanted to raise goats, so having more land and our own place will be wonderful."

"You mean you have not always dreamed of being in service to the king as a tax collector?" asked Sam. The minute he said it, the builder regretted his words. Marcus rarely spoke of his personal life, and he was disliked by some solely on account of his job.

"It is a good-paying job," Marcus said stiffly. "We all owe the king for his protection and services. He staffs the army that protects us, paves the roads we travel on, and maintains the aqueducts built to provide our water. Working for the king is an honorable job."

"Of course, Marcus." Sam felt his heart sink. "Please forgive me. My attempt at humor was not well thought out. Your position is indeed necessary in the kingdom. I admit there were times when I felt resentment for the money I had to pay, but…" He felt himself stumbling over a moment that could have been a wonderful opportunity to ask Marcus about his hopes and dreams…and perhaps his faith. Sam tried to get back on solid footing. "But that is not what is important, is it? Today we will plan your new house and how it will be constructed in a way that keeps the goats away from your wife's vegetables, yes?"

Marcus managed a smile, and Sam felt the tension ease. "My crew and I will create a fine new cottage you and your wife will love." Turning to face his crew, he unexpectedly noticed that the men looked embarrassed and some even seemed sad. The crewmen looked down and wouldn't meet his gaze. Sam was puzzled.

"Men, what's wrong? Surely you will agree to build Marcus's house?" he asked.

"Foreman Sam," Thomas said, "we would all like to work with you on this next project. We've wanted to talk to you about the coming work, but Grecco said to leave it up to him. But since he hasn't yet, I will tell you that he assigned all of us to another team. Because you didn't have contracts coming up, he wanted to make sure we had work."

Sam was quiet for a long time. Finally he said, "I understand, Thomas. But are there some here who are willing to work as part of my crew?" Sam looked at the men hopefully.

"We would all gladly work with you again, Sam," replied Thomas. "But you need to speak to Grecco about it."

Sam felt his calm being replaced by anxiety. Still, he summoned his voice and announced, "Okay. I will work out the details with Grecco. Marcus, I will meet with you on Monday with a crew to begin your house. Men of my crew, thank you and God bless you for helping me create this beautiful, well-built house. We have done what we set out to do. We have constructed a place where a family can live and love and prosper. This has been a good project."

And with that the crew started packing up their tools. With

an anxious heart full of doubt, Sam walked down the street and headed to the building site across town where Grecco was overseeing some repairs to the walls of the blacksmith's workshop.

"Sam, I was going to visit you at your home this evening," Grecco said as he reached out to shake hands with his foreman.

Sam took Grecco's hand firmly and responded, "Then I'm happy I've saved you a trip. My crew and I have finished the house, and we're ready to move on. The tax collector has asked that our next job be a house for him, and I've heard that several other people have inquired about having my crew and me work on their upcoming projects."

"I *am* pleased with all I'm hearing, Sam," Grecco agreed. He motioned for Sam to step aside so they could speak more privately. "But, Sam, previous to this last job, your work was suffering greatly. Because of that, and because you didn't have any contracts lined up, I had to make some difficult decisions. Your work on the last project was exemplary, but because of your work before that, I have to release you from your foreman duties. I know you are a good worker, so I don't want to lose you. I'd like to assign you to John the Elder's crew. He's an excellent foreman who promotes the same values and work ethics you demonstrated in your last project. I'm sure you'll work well with him, and I'm confident he can learn from you too."

"I–I–I don't understand," Sam said, his cheery demeanor clouding over. "Did not the last project exceed everyone's expectations? You yourself admitted the work we did was exemplary. And yet you're demoting me...assigning my crew to others and asking me to work on John the Elder's crew?"

Grecco put his hand on Sam's shoulder. "I made this decision awhile ago, Sam. I hoped for a long time that you would get back on track, but when you didn't I knew I had to make some changes. I waited until this last house was finished because I didn't want the work to suffer or to take you off a project before it was completed." Grecco's eyes were kind. "You know I think long and hard when I make decisions. I consider the work to be done, the customers' expectations, the well-being and skill of the crews, and the financial ramifications. And I think about the effects my decisions will have on the people who work for me, even down to the individuals, including you, Sam.

"For the past few years I have observed your leadership skills deteriorate and your work quality decline. Your hastily built projects caused growing dissatisfaction from our customers. I also watched as you changed your sense of worth to one based on accumulating money instead of serving the customer and providing the best quality service possible. I know what you can do, Sam. And I still believe in your talents and abilities—"

"Grecco, please don't do this. I know my work and leadership went downhill, but I've changed. I recognized the same things you did, and I've set about to change them. I've rededicated myself to God, and opened my heart and mind to His leading. My priorities have changed, and I'm once again excited about working hard, doing my best, and offering the best service I can. I've never felt more ready to lead than I do right now."

Grecco looked into Sam's eyes. "If what you say is true, then now is the perfect time for you to serve by working on John the Elder's crew."

"Grecco, please believe me—"

"I do believe you, Sam. I see you've turned your life around for the better in the last few months. But I also know a person can find it easy to change when times get tough and life isn't working out as he or she planned. And when we're searching for a way out of the darkness, God's light is beautiful and uplifting. But after the initial glow wears down and life resumes its grinding pace, will we continue to seek God's ways or fall back into our old habits? Will we follow God when the glow of success once again lights our path? That is the true test, Sam. And that takes time.

"Yes, I do believe you are changing and making positive strides forward. And the last project went very well. But it can't erase the work you did the last few years. There are too many people who are hesitant about working for you or hiring you. People evaluate people by the habits and attitudes that have been established, and it takes time to overcome the negative perceptions. One successful project isn't enough to counter the many projects that were done haphazardly. If I didn't care for you so much and have confidence in your abilities, and if your work hadn't improved so there have been recent requests for your services, you wouldn't have a job right now. And your membership in the Builders Guild would be in question."

"How can I live on a crewman's pay? I've made decisions based on my pay as a foreman and on the knowledge that people have again requested my crew for their projects. How can I go back to being just a worker on a crew?" Sam couldn't hide his overwhelming shame and sense of failure. He shook his head, and finally covered his eyes by rubbing his brow with both hands.

"You may be more dependent on your past desires, habits, and perceptions of success than you know, Sam. They take great effort and time to change. I understand that it is very difficult to lose a position of prominence. But I'm hoping you'll accept this change with good grace. And if your work and attitude continues as it has been for the last job, there's no reason why you can't attain a foreman position again in the future. What will you choose to do, Sam? Will you continue to work for me by joining John the Elder's crew?"

"This is very hard, Grecco. I'm not sure what to do."

"It takes courage to accept the consequences of some of our choices, does it not? Especially when the changes can be seen by others. But you can do it, Sam. And you will be a better person for it." Grecco paused and then returned to his firm stance. "Returning to crew, you'll have to learn to live according to your means, as we all do. But one plus is that you'll earn a guaranteed wage every week, which will make it easier to budget. Surely that will help." Grecco paused again and looked Sam in the eye. "Monday morning, you can meet up with John and his crew at the building site of Marcus the tax collector's new house. I'll take care of telling Marcus about the change in foremen. May I tell John to expect you?"

"Yes, Grecco, I'll be there."

"Sam, that's a wise decision. I'm glad you're going to stay and work with me and my company."

At home, Sam sat in deep thought and prayer before the hearth fire. He was interrupted by a small, sweet voice.

"Daddy, why is your face so sad?"

His four-year-old daughter with a mop of curly dark hair took Sam's face between her two little hands and turned it toward her own serious face.

Sam managed a wan smile. "I'm not really sad, Mary. I'm praying to God and thinking very hard. I'm trying to figure out what to do about a problem."

"May I help you, Daddy?" Little Mary cocked her head to one side, her eyes brightening with interest.

"No, my small child, you can't." Speaking more to himself, Sam looked up to the ceiling and added, "Sometimes what we've done in the past affects what's going to happen. I made some mistakes that I have to fix. I drove myself away from my work."

"You drove yourself where, Daddy?" Two insistent hands pulled Sam's face and gaze back down.

Sam took the hands, kissed them, and softly laughed. "Nowhere, honey. I guess you could say I was given the boot!" He smiled at Mary's solemn face.

Mary stared at her father's eyes. Then a smile of glowing insight and hope spread across her young face. She chirped happily, "Then you should go see Magowin!"

Sam was astonished. "Mary, you are a helpful child! Why do you say I should go see Magowin the cobbler?"

Mary brimmed with pride at having helped her daddy. She stood straight and said, "So you can get the other boot!"

The next day...

Sam and Magowin sat in the warm, familiar shoe shop sharing a bowl of walnuts.

"I was so embarrassed, Magowin. I spoke without thinking to Marcus. Even though I didn't intend to, I insulted him. How could I have done that? I thought my heart had changed. Instead, I regressed. And now I find that I have been demoted to crewman. And I won't have a chance to become a foreman until next autumn. Magowin, the joy and confidence I felt just two days ago have disappeared. Why? Why has this happened now when I rededicated my love and life to God and have been working toward living by His principles that are found in your laws of true prosperity?"

Magowin cleared some shells from the bowl. "They are not *my* laws, Sam."

"No, not yours. But these laws on achieving true prosperity—where have they brought me? I put my heart and soul into my work. I felt fully alive for the first time in a long time only to find that my past mistakes have come back to haunt me. This shame is too much," Sam said as tears formed in his eyes. "I don't understand why I'm being punished. I don't understand why God is allowing this now."

"And you need to understand?"

Sam looked at Magowin. "Yes, I do need to understand. I want to know why God is allowing this to happen when I'm praying and thanking Him and working hard to live and follow the path He's showing me. What happened to true prosperity? Ha! For this I must suffer such indignation, such embarrassment? I have lost hope, Magowin."

"That is a sad statement," the old cobbler said. "But, my kind friend, these events do indeed reveal how the Creator works. Your attitude and reaction to adversity reveal less about God than they do about you. You are trusting your own perceptions on these matters so strongly that you feel justified for being angry at God. Yet you've admitted to concerns about holding on to your faith."

"What do you mean?"

"Do you remember after we took a load of your wood to the young widow's house? After you had talked to God in the forest? You came back a rich man that day, did you not? You had tapped into and experienced the wisdom of the Divine's truth. You were filled with amazing certainty that day—a glowing, radiant certainty. And you've experienced similar moments all along this new journey of yours. And each time it buoys you, yes? It reminds you that God loves you and wants you to work with Him to achieve His purposes and goals through the dreams He gives you."

"Magowin, please. I'm feeling foolish enough already. I'm not sure I'm following you."

"You're not foolish, Sam. Confused, perhaps. You misjudged your thoughts. That day you asked me how you could hold on to this feeling, this sure knowing, this confidence. You said you were but a man with many faults so you didn't know if you could hang on. Do you remember asking me about this?"

Sam sighed. "I remember."

"The truth is that you can't hold on to those wondrous moments of inspiration."

"But I thought…"

"That's right. *You* thought. You thought you could be in control of this new spiritual path. You thought you could arrange it so you would always feel safely wrapped in God's loving arms, communing with His Spirit. You thought you could stay aloft on your terms, released from the life of humans on this earth, released from the material greed and temptations to sin that fill this earth. You thought by creating a new life open to divine inspiration, generosity, and love for others you could escape any errors or sins from the past."

"I still don't understand. You said if I followed the laws—"

"And you have, Sam. You have followed the laws you know so far. And God has rewarded you with the perfect circumstances to achieve your dreams."

"No, He hasn't."

"Ah, Sam, that is the crux, isn't it? Is that what *you* think or what God thinks?"

"How can I know what God thinks?"

"I'm so glad you finally asked!" Magowin sat back and smiled. "We can never fully know what God thinks, but we can study what He tells us in His Word, we can learn from those who live by His teachings, and we can partner with the Holy Spirit to shape our feelings and thoughts by His wisdom so we begin to feel and think as He does. And we can only begin to understand what God feels and thinks by experiencing life with our soul, our heart, our eyes, our ears, and—" Magowin tapped his chest and then his head. "And with our heart and mind open."

"I should have a heart and mind that are open to having my dreams shattered or shoved in my face?"

"That is *your* perception, Sam. *Your* reality. That is how *you* are choosing to view this development. My perception and reality and thoughts are not the same as yours. And neither are God's."

"That's because you and God are not suffering this humiliation."

Magowin leaned forward. "Jesus suffered the ultimate humiliation of death on a cross for our benefit, Sam. And I have suffered through my own heartaches. I've endured things I do not wish on anyone. You have lost a foreman's position, Sam. I lost my beloved wife, my Sarah, a fascinating woman with laughter like bells, a talent for cooking, and a trusting heart. For three long years after she died I lost my will to follow God's urgings. For three long years I allowed myself to wallow in a false, dark reality. But for the faith of my dear wife, I would not have come out of that dark time. You are not alone in having experienced confusion." Magowin's eyes, although filled with tears, were serene.

Sam leaned back and stared at Magowin, waiting for him to explain.

"The reason my perception is different," Magowin continued, "is not that I am holier than you, Sam, or because God loves me more or in a different way than He does you. My perception is different because I have spent many, many years seeking God and His wisdom, allowing Him to live through me while I lived through Him. I have a maturity in my faith that you have yet to attain. Through the years I've allowed the Divine to shape my thoughts, my habits, my attitudes. Because of this, I can often look beyond the present circumstance to see how God is using them for change. When I encounter what I used to refer to as setbacks, I now pray, 'God, this is difficult. What do You want me to learn from this situation?'

"I have learned that He works on a 'need to know' basis, and that in His right timing the Holy Spirit will give me the knowledge I need for that time in my life. And through these experiences with God, my faith in Him is now such that I am often rewarded with a miraculous, ever-growing sense of understanding that is beyond my human capability. And this is just as satisfying as the head-spinning bursts of joy I feel when I experience divine inspiration or insights and fall to my knees in praise. You know what I mean by those dizzying moments, do you not?"

Sam nodded. "Yes, those moments when the path is made clear, when truth fills our being. But I don't feel anything like that now."

"Worry not. Those moments will continue to bless you in the future. I promise you that because I know God." Magowin smiled. "Our God knows how much we need that encouragement and how much they motivate us. But He also knows they can't sustain us. That we can't hold on to those intense moments."

"So where is God now? His presence seems to vanish. Even though I'm following Him, praying to Him, and following His principles, He doesn't seem to be responding."

"You have yet to learn and follow the fifth law."

"The fifth? I have already failed, and I'm trying to follow only four laws. How can I even think of trying to follow a fifth?" Sam asked.

"You have *not* failed, Sam. That's *your* perception—*your* attitude, *your* voice, *your* mindset. Let's try to view it from God's perspective."

Sam looked up, readying his hardened heart to hear a lecture on finding the best in everything. But Magowin's wise, understanding eyes softened Sam's heart, and he found himself asking, "What do you see from God's point of view?"

"I see that your fine work on this last project saved you from being fired altogether. True?"

"Yes, that's true," Sam admitted grudgingly.

"I see that you have been given all that you prayed for."

"No. No, I haven't. Not at all."

"Yes, you have, Sam. You will still be in the construction trade, and that is your dream, yes? You will still be loving others through your work, yes?"

"Well, okay, I can see that," Sam conceded.

"And the best part is that for at least a year you can successfully budget and set up a wise financial plan because you'll know exactly what your income will be month to month."

"I earned more as a foreman..."

"You haven't lately," Magowin corrected.

"But I did for a while. And I could again."

"And risk slipping back into the same habits you had before? The desire for more and more possessions and prestige that eventually led to so much anxiety and pain?"

"No, I wouldn't go back to that. I've changed!"

"If you've changed, why does this change in circumstance upset you so?"

"You don't understand, Magowin," Sam said bitterly.

Magowin's voice was firm. "I *do* understand. What you're distressed about is your loss of position. And perhaps your loss of power. Your dependence on this prestige will keep you from achieving true success, true freedom, and true abundance. As long as you rely on a title or position for your value and place on this earth, you are not relying on God or seeing yourself through His eyes. You're no better off than when you relied on financial and material accumulation. Examine your heart, Sam, and you'll see that my words are true."

Sam eyed Magowin. Everything he said was true.

Very slowly, very gently, Magowin continued. "My friend, you are not being punished. You want God to save you from the consequences of your actions, but God doesn't always work like that. He allows the consequences to continue to help you understand how His ways are different than yours, and your ways are different than His. Thankfully, God does not leave us alone during this time. He gives us the strength to persevere through the testing. He allows us to see what we have done with His help to encourage us. And

He is merciful and gracious and doesn't allow us to face anything we can't handle. He always provides His great assistance or a way out of the difficulty. Are you understanding what I'm saying, Sam?"

"I think so…"

"You have helped create a beautiful new house for folks who needed some love. Wouldn't you say that you and Suzette have drawn closer together lately?"

"Yes, we have done that," Sam said.

"You have experienced the joy of giving. You have felt the energy that comes from loving your work and loving others through your work. That is part of God's way. You have much to encourage you to go forward on. And through this adversity or difficulty you are facing, you have a very wonderful opportunity to grow. Deep inside, I know you are praying fervently for understanding."

Sam whispered humbly, "Am I?"

"This despair, this pit, this frustration with God you give voice to is actually a heartfelt prayer that is echoing through the halls of heaven as we speak." Magowin smiled gently at Sam. "You are saying, 'God, please tell me why this is happening.' And He will, Sam. He will. For you have advanced to the fifth law."

"But I feel like I've gone backward, not forward."

"Sometimes it does feel that way. Sometimes before a time of change—when we are realizing our old habits and old ways of living and thinking will not work for us anymore—we feel afraid and even angry. But it is at these times that growth is about to take place. This is your chance to approach your life in a whole new way. This is your chance to let go of the fear you have that others will think less of you, that they will see you and think, 'Aha! Once a wood gatherer, always a wood gatherer—'"

Sam turned pale and tears welled in his eyes. "Magowin, h–h– how do you know this? I could not bear to speak it inside my head, much less say it out loud."

"Because I love you, Sam. I love you through God's eyes. And I have faith that as you mature in your faith and study God's Word, you will see through God's eyes more and more. And that is actually what you are seeking, Sam. That's the fifth law. The *Law of Understanding* is understanding your fears and what holds you back. You may believe in God's wisdom, you may prioritize, you may love others, and you may be generous, but until you are tested, until you face adversity, you will not fully understand how your viewpoint is so very different than God's, how your perspective is so limited to the immediate circumstance, but God's perspective is not only here and now but also long term.

"That this understanding is often revealed through despairing and harrowing situations often comes as a surprise. Even the devout experience hard times and struggle to understand God's will and purposes for the pain and struggles we experience and see all around us. I struggle with this at times even now. Don't be too hard on yourself during this time, Sam. This Law of Understanding can be intimidating. It teaches that the goal of a genuinely successful life is to stay on God's path and seek to think and love and see as He does. Through ever-increasing understanding, you will experience more wonder and more abundance."

"But that will take forever."

"Precisely. This is the path of all who seek to be holy." Magowin chuckled. "Hey, I like that!"

"This path is for people who seek no earthly riches, for those who require no guaranteed income. But, Magowin, I must live as a worker. I am not like Pastor Wright, who can spend his days in study and prayer. I have a family who needs a home and food. I–I like this law, but surely a man such as I…"

"A man such as you is as beloved to God as anyone else. God wants you to know Him. When you set your foot on the path to understanding, He will provide the teachers and moments of inspiration. He sent His Holy Spirit to partner with you. Your job is to seek to understand God's ways and thoughts. And when they have been made clear, to follow them with God's help. And as you do, you will change…not through your own efforts but via a partnership with God. You will begin to understand and view situations as He does, little by little at first." Magowin paused, obviously in thought. Then he said, "Sam, you are indeed a fortunate man! Why do I say this? Because the first step you will take toward pursuing this lifelong Law of Understanding is clear!"

"It is?"

"Oh yes! You need to learn to read."

Sam stared at him for a few seconds before the shock wore off and he could protest.

Magowin held up his hand. "You forget that I know a bit about how you think. No matter what you say, I know why you have not learned to read. You thought you would appear to be a simple, foolish woodsman. You were afraid you might fail. Better to stay the course than to fail, yes? To contemplate the holy writings in your own meditative silence, you must learn to read them for yourself, Sam. I encourage you to go to Pastor Wright. He will be willing to teach you. He can also direct you to other great writings that were written under the inspiration of the Holy Spirit. Your world is about to open up, Sam. You will be in wonder, and you will crave even more understanding. This is an exciting time in your life, Sam!"

Magowin's enthusiasm was contagious. Sam felt his spirit lighten as hope flooded his heart.

"And Pastor Wright will also teach you about the sixth law."

"Pastor Wright will? What is the sixth law?"

"The sixth law says that we must plan and set wise goals for personal, financial, and business management."

"But Magowin!" Sam exclaimed, taken aback. "I know Pastor

Wright has much to teach me about spiritual matters, but what can he teach me about budgets and planning? How can a man who has so little money teach me about financial management?"

"Good question, Sam! You have opened your mind to another matter in which you require understanding."

Sam groaned. "This is going to be a very long year," he complained good-naturedly.

"Ah, that reminds me!" Magowin jumped from his chair. As sprightly as a young boy, he skipped back to the corner of his shop and returned holding a package. "It is also going to be a cold, wet year, according to the widow Williams. And I find much wisdom from Mrs. Williams, I can tell you." Magowin unwrapped the paper and held out a brand-new, superbly stitched pair of lined leather boots freshly rubbed with oil. "These are for you as payment for helping me last month. There will be days you must work in the damp. May these boots keep you warm and dry!"

Sam held the boots up, and his laughter burst forth.

Magowin paused, puzzled. "Why are you laughing?" he asked.

All Sam could do was sputter between his hoots of joyful amazement. Finally he got out what he wanted to say. "Because you're so right, Magowin! There's much I have yet to understand. It's a long story, but my four-year-old told me to come to you to get a boot, and so I have! If my little daughter can teach me, then maybe there's hope for me yet. Yes, there is much hope!"

11

Making Adjustments

The next week was indeed cold and wet. Each day Sam walked the mile to the building site for Marcus's new house wearing his new, sturdy work boots. He reported to John the Elder. Although Sam felt awkward at first, he soon relaxed because the men accepted him in his new role without any fuss. And when he took on the work he was assigned without complaint and diligently did his best, the men admired him even more. Although Sam wasn't aware of it, his positive attitude and humility were also noted by John the Elder and reported to Grecco.

Each day Sam and the other tradesmen worried they would be sent home due to the bad weather conditions. But they weren't. Instead, John the Elder took the initiative to turn the wet, slushy days into creative opportunities. Every morning with good humor, he announced to the crew that even though the bad weather wouldn't permit the usual timber work, it wouldn't deter their progress.

"We're going to divide into two crews while it rains," John explained. "One crew will gather stones from the creek bed and sort them according to size for either the chimney or foundation. The other crew will dig rocks from the garden site to use for terracing so the good soil won't wash away during the rains. If it keeps raining, we'll finish the terracing, notice where the rainwater flows, and construct runoff channels to keep the gardens from becoming saturated and lead the water to other planting areas. When the skies are clear, we'll work on the house. Thankfully there is much we can do even in this drizzle!"

On the third day of terracing and garden preparation, a mason said, "John, I've wielded a pick for three days now. Are these gardens part of the contract? I'm not a landscaper; I'm a mason."

"We are more than builders of buildings and gardens. We're builders of homes and dreams," John countered with a smile. "We know Marcus's wife loves to garden, do we not? We know this house will need a hearth and chimney, yes? We also know that staying home during the rainy days will delay our progress and cut into our pay. By unearthing and gathering these stones, we save our customers from having to buy bricks for the chimney and foundation. By preparing these garden beds, we know that crops will be grown that we may be able to buy and enjoy. By attending to these details, we are adding value to the house and delighting our customers. Would you rather stay home and miss these opportunities?"

"No, I guess not," the mason replied.

Sam overheard the conversation, and he nodded in approval. Grecco had been correct. John the Elder was a foreman whose heart was in his work and whose instruction was valuable and uplifting. In his new boots, in his new position, and with a renewed heart, Sam enjoyed the physical labor as the misty gray days allowed the workers to turn part of Marcus's house site into a gardener's paradise.

After two weeks, the gardens were complete, the house foundation had been laid and constructed, and timbers had been hewn for the frame. Marcus and his wife were excited about the progress. Although they offered praise when they saw the wonderful gardens and terraced walkways that had been laid out, they were a little concerned too.

"John," asked Marcus quietly, "how are we to pay for all this extra work? We don't have—"

"The contract remains the same, Marcus," John cut in. "If a stone hearth and chimney are acceptable, we have saved quite a bit of money by not having to order brick. That will cover the extra work we've done."

"Yes, they are!" Marcus exclaimed.

"Very well then. Just remember us next year when the turnips and berries are ripe!" John smiled broadly and turned back to his work.

And payday arrived…

Sam sat across from Suzette that evening with two weeks worth of wages piled on the table. "This is all I will be bringing home each fortnight. It doesn't seem like much."

"It's plenty," responded Suzette. "We'll live quite well on the income from our work."

"And we'll continue to give generously," Sam reminded Suzette gently.

"Yes, we will!"

"I t–think w–we would do much b–better and be able to live more simply if we m–moved to a house more suited to our needs," Sam said hesitantly.

Suzette placed her hands on Sam's. "Are you saying we can finally live in the cozy little home of our dreams? I've had my eye on that cottage on the market square—you know, the one I've always adored with the large window with shutters in the front? I've heard it's going to be sold soon. Sam, surely we can sell this large house and find happiness in that beautiful house. I can picture us there, Sam. I've always seen us living in the bustling town center where folks can pass by and smell my gooseberry pies cooling in the window."

"And view your curtains and dresses and cloth wares," Sam added with a knowing, loving smile.

Suzette returned his smile. "It would be a perfect place for us."

"The cottage is to be sold? The widow Williams' house? She hasn't taken ill, has she?"

"Not at all! She is to be married. Magowin has proposed. Isn't that wonderful?"

Sam continued to listen in peaceful amazement to Suzette's positive comments about downsizing. Instead of feeling devastated about giving up this fine, expensive house, Suzette was vibrant with hope and excitement. And he too felt happy because of his secure understanding that prayers were being answered all around him. "That is blessed news about Magowin. Blessed, blessed news. He hinted about this to me a long time ago, but I was too preoccupied with my own problems to pick up on his excitement. I think this is wonderful news! This is a win–win situation since the widow's place would be a great house for us. I'll talk to Geoffrey tomorrow about selling this house and buying that one. After I take our tithe to Pastor Wright, that is," Sam said.

"I've brought a contribution to the church's work, Pastor Wright," Sam said as he handed over a small pouch of coins. "Suzette tells me the reading classes are underway and going well."

"Bless you and thank you! Come in, my man, come in. Share these biscuits and fresh butter with me." Pastor Wright led Sam into a small study with walls lined with books and stacks of papers. It smelled of old bindings—the comforting, intriguing smell of knowledge new and ancient.

"Your family has added much to this church and community, Sam. Suzette has started a class for the younger readers, and I'm teaching the older ones. Your eldest daughter, Martha, helps with the youngest. She's so like a young lady, isn't she? And the money you've given has enabled me to buy books, writing supplies, and desks. We have been so richly blessed as the church took on this reading program for the children in our community."

"So much already?" Sam was pleasantly amazed.

Pastor Wright smiled. "I'm very careful with budgeting, and I'm good at finding bargains. Here, try this biscuit."

Sam sat down and enjoyed the cozy room and delicious, buttery biscuits. Taking in the vast number of volumes around him—volumes he was sure were filled with age-old wisdom, new ideas, and information about history, philosophy, and poetry. He knew that now was the time to admit one of his deepest secrets and share a dream of his heart.

"Um…" started Sam. "Pastor, I was wondering… Well, I—I was hoping you might be willing to instruct me on how to—"

"Develop a financial plan?" Pastor Wright quickly offered.

An awkward pause seemed to go on forever until Sam finally got more words out. "I…no…um, excuse me. What made you say that?"

"I advise and guide many couples and singles on sound financial planning and money management. It's part of my job."

"It is?"

"Certainly. The spiritual well-being of every parishioner is my utmost concern. And I know that poverty and lack of financial priorities and planning contribute to great unhappiness and help sidetrack godly values."

"So you teach people about handling money?"

"Oh yes! It's imperative to handle our finances wisely, don't you think?"

"Yes. But if you will excuse me for asking, how much do you know about finances? What I mean is, well, you live on a limited budget, so why are you qualified to give advice on money matters?"

"Could there be a better person, Sam? The fact that I live quite happily within my means—even below my means so I can share with others and save for emergencies—should be proof that it can be done. And in case you think my position as a minister enables me—directs me—to have a financially disciplined and generous spirit, I offer this to consider. Perhaps it was my disciplined, contented, and generous spirit that led me to my career."

Sam listened and now viewed his pastor in a new light.

"Do you know why I wanted to teach the children to read?" the pastor asked. Without waiting for an answer, he continued. "Because they will find greater happiness and closeness to God when they can read His Word for themselves. Do you know why I teach people to budget and plan? Because they will find greater happiness and closeness to God when they are free to follow their callings without the restraint of debt, overabundance of material possessions, and financial confusion. If a parishioner is poor but finds happiness—true happiness—in his work, he must still budget, tithe, and save. He may have very little materially, but he will be rich in spirit. Even the wealthy must practice sound financial planning to stay on top of their priorities and goals. Sometimes it's the wealthy who need the most instruction because their resources are a responsibility that can easily chain them down. They too need to find freedom so they can walk more closely with God."

"You're right, pastor. I haven't given this much thought. I never realized this was part of your…your…"

"Mission," the pastor supplied with a gentle smile.

Sam was struck by the seriousness in the pastor's youthful eyes. "We are fortunate to have you in our town and church, pastor."

Pastor Wright leaned back. "I know you've taken a…a new position working with John the Elder's crew. I thought perhaps you might need a bit of help with money matters." Pastor Wright looked intently into Sam's eyes. "Some planning and preparation guidance. It seems reasonable."

Sam felt a cool, easy breath go into his body as he inhaled

and then relaxed a bit. "I do need your instruction, Pastor Wright. But not because I'm in a mess. Rather, Suzette and I are starting on a very joy-filled path. We've already decided to sell our large house and buy a much cozier one to decrease our financial burden. I'm committed to working hard no matter what position I hold. Suzette is dedicated to doing her needlework. And we are both committed to our children. And God is the source of our strength and joy. We are blessed to tithe and go beyond that to help people who need it. We have purposed to use our money wisely. I've made mistakes in the past, and I made some foolish investments and purchased on credit. I've been very good at handling budgets for building projects, but when it comes to personal finance, I—"

"When it comes to our own finances, it can be difficult, can't it?" the pastor said. "Have you and Suzette established some short- and long-term goals and plans?"

"Not really. We've started working on priorities, but we haven't tackled finances in that way. I know we should, but…"

"*Why* should you?"

"What do you mean?" Sam asked.

"What I'm asking, Sam, is why do you think you *should* consider financial planning?"

"So we can live within our means and avoid going into debt."

Pastor Wright scrunched his face. "Yuck! What drudgery. Surely there must be a more exciting and motivating reason?"

"Pastor Wright, you are confusing me like Magowin does at times."

"Magowin! He is a character, isn't he?" The pastor grinned. "He came by to see me the other day."

"To ask about a wedding ceremony?" Sam guessed.

"There are no secrets in this town. Yes, he's planning to marry. What a happy occasion that's going to be. He is a beloved man and a special cobbler. Aren't we lucky he makes our shoes?"

"Yes we are," Sam agreed. "And he's always so generous."

"Precisely! Magowin lives well *below* his means so he can make his living as a cobbler, which he enjoys, and have enough money and free time to help those in need and minister to people who seek his counsel. Without careful financial planning and budgeting, he wouldn't be able to do this. Did you know that about Magowin?"

"I haven't asked about his finances, Pastor Wright. We haven't really discussed money."

"What I meant to ask is, do you know that without careful financial preparation you can't live your dreams responsibly, completely, and with true freedom?"

"Yes, I do know that. Isn't that what I said before?"

"Not exactly. You said you needed to adhere to a financial plan so you can live *within* your means and *avoid* debt."

Sam was silent as he considered the difference Pastor Wright was pointing out. "Okay, I see what you're saying. Living within my means and avoiding debt aren't actual goals. My true goal is to walk with God, serving Him during this life so my heart, mind, and energy can go into my family I love, my work I enjoy, and the people I can help. And to follow these goals, I need to live within my means and avoid debt because that will help me serve God even more and experience freedom and joy daily."

"Amen, my brother. You are more in tune than many people I know. I can see you're already on the path to a life filled with love, happiness, perseverance, and meaning. You must already know many of the laws of true prosperity."

Sam sat tall. "I'm still working on incorporating the laws into my life and work. Magowin has been enlightening me, and I've been talking to God and listening to your Bible teachings to gain God's wisdom. Pastor Wright, you're a spiritual man, so you will understand my heart." Sam paused to collect his thoughts. "When I first walked into Magowin's shop, I was filled with anxiety and a desire for money. I wasn't even there to ask Magowin for help or wisdom. I was seeking the whereabouts of Geoffrey the money-lender. I was consumed with fear of losing my grip on wealth. As you know, I once held a position of authority and earned quite a bit of money…"

"I remember," Pastor Wright said.

"But now I understand material wealth doesn't bring happiness. These laws—the seven laws of true prosperity Magowin and others have been teaching me—are really principles on how to live with a full heart and find prosperity according to God's view and within His arms. I went into Magowin's shop seeking the moneylender so I could borrow more money to try to get back my wealth and fill the emptiness inside. But now I sit before you as a man who knows money and possessions can never fill the void in my soul. I sit before you as a man who enjoys life by following God and looking forward to more blessings as He allows me to live and work meaningfully and help the people around me. I seek the understanding and wisdom of God instead of financial riches. And God is blessing me beyond what I ever imagined!"

"Ah, you are at the fifth law, the Law of Understanding," mused the pastor. "This quest for understanding is a lifelong one. It's a life-filling, soul-filling, longstanding openness to God's will and His ways."

"That's another reason I'm here, Pastor Wright. In discovering more about this Law of Understanding, something I've kept secret for a long time has come up. Although I'm good with numbers and do calculations for work, I can't read words. I've been so embarrassed about this, but I want to learn to read. Will you teach me? I could ask Suzette, but I think it might be better to learn from someone else. Magowin suggested I ask you. I—"

"Say no more, Sam. I understand. I'll be glad to help you. And when you've progressed a ways, you may feel more comfortable asking Suzette to help you too."

"Thank you, pastor. When can we start?"

"This is going to be an absolute pleasure. Not only will you learn to read, but this will give us opportunities to discuss God and His ways. You might be surprised to learn that I too am constantly seeking to improve my understanding and awareness of God, His thoughts, and His ways. I'm always looking for insights for sharing with others the light of God's love and truth."

"Then I will learn to read, and together you and I can discover more about God," Sam said with enthusiasm.

12

Dreaming Again

After discussing with Sam methods for learning how to read, Pastor Wright leaned forward. "There is one more thing. I'm delighted to help you learn to read, but will you also allow me to help you with your finances?"

"Why?" Sam asked. "By selling our house and moving into a more affordable one, we're obviously reducing our expenses. Doesn't that show we're being prudent with our money? We're also tithing regularly plus giving when we see someone we can help."

"Do you feel content about your future?"

"Yes, I do." Sam beamed.

"But not particularly excited?"

"Excited? Well, in a way, I suppose I am. Suzette is excited, this I'm sure of."

"Is it because money won't be so tight? Will her life be easier or simpler?"

Sam laughed. "I'm not sure of that. Suzette stays very busy. She's very happy when she's taking care of the children and working on her embroidery and stitching. She somehow manages to attend to the home and the children and her work while maintaining a joyful, calm attitude. More so than I do."

"And she teaches a reading class."

"She's always taught the children, including the neighbor children at times. I can't see her life getting simpler by our move. In fact, we're thinking of purchasing the widow Williams's cottage house because it has a large window that opens onto the market square. My wife is a businesswoman, you know—"

"One of the best," acknowledged the pastor. "How much better our town would be if everyone approached his or her work with the same care and love. I wouldn't be surprised if Suzette had bigger dreams for her seamstress business, especially now that the children are older. I'm sure your eldest daughter, Martha, watches the other two at times now."

Sam's eyes twinkled. "You do know my wife!"

"And I know you, Sam."

"Me? In what way?"

"I know you have dreams of a brighter future."

"I did, Pastor Wright. But now I'm no longer interested in furthering my career. That's why I don't understand why we need to study finances. I'd rather study the Scriptures and spend more time in prayer. I'm quite content to love my family, be a crewman, serve my community, and gain more understanding about God and His ways."

"So you would deprive our town of your gifts?"

"I don't understand the question. No matter how small our income, Suzette and I will tithe and help people. I will continue to serve people through my work as a crewman."

Pastor Wright looked intently at Sam. "Your words *sound* noble, but I'm wondering if that's what your heart is saying. Do you feel you've become the person God meant for you to be when He gave you the dreams that resulted in your moving to town?"

"So much has happened in the last few months, pastor. Your question is difficult to answer. I do know I never again want to live without talking to God and listening to His voice. I want to understand and follow His ways. Is this what I dreamed of? I believe so. When I felt lifted and inspired, I knew God was with me. But when I let my attention turn to accumulating money and possessions, envy and jealousy took over. Eventually I felt empty inside." Sam looked at his hands. "So, yes, who I am becoming is who I dreamed of being because I am with God and living more and more for Him."

"So you're telling me that once you became prosperous and successful you left God out of the picture?"

"I know I did."

"So you associate success and prosperity with unhappiness and emptiness?"

Sam laughed softly. "Now I do. I certainly didn't always feel and think that way though."

"You can be one of the best foremen in this town, Sam."

A great heaviness fell on Sam, and pain crept into his voice. "Pastor Wright, I can't think about such a thing. After I went down that road I thought I couldn't bear to face God again, but I finally did. I thought I lost my ability to feel love for people and put them first, but now I do. I thought I couldn't humble myself before a cobbler or before my wife or before the men I work with without dying, but I did because God gave me the strength. I thought I couldn't bear the humiliation of stepping down from an important job I loved and took pride in, but now I have found peace and understanding. I thought my house and possessions defined me, but now I am rid of that burden. I have always been ashamed I couldn't learn to read. I was too embarrassed to ask to be taught. But here I am asking you to help me. There is so much I am free of and free to do. Why do you ask me about old dreams? I'm no longer a foreman, and that is as it should be. I let my old life corrupt my heart and lead me away from God. Now I am free and content. My definition of prosperity no longer includes desiring money."

"So you don't intend to listen to God?"

Sam was aghast. "What do you mean?"

"Was it not God who opened your heart to new possibilities and dreams? Was it not the Holy Spirit who filled you with the desire and drive to lead your crew to build such a good house last month with the extra touches that made it really special? When you finished that job, did you praise God?"

"Yes, of course! He was with us every day, inspiring us and giving us joy. My heart was filled with His Spirit every day. But I let success go to my head, and now I'm paying the consequences. So I am happy to serve on John the Elder's crew. He brings wisdom and love to his work and encourages us to do the same. I am free of the desire to obtain prestige."

"You are afraid."

Sam was shocked at the pastor's simple statement. "Afraid? Of course not. What would I be afraid of? I am content being an honest man doing honorable work. As long as I'm careful of what I dream of and make sure I handle our money well, I'm okay. What does it matter if I'm but a simple construction worker?"

"You are afraid, Sam," the pastor repeated.

"I just got *over* being afraid," Sam countered. "Why do you say I'm afraid?"

"You're afraid to follow your dreams. You are afraid that if you were once again in a position of authority you would fall into temptation again. You are afraid that if you are very successful, especially financially, you would once again fail. Is this not true?"

"I don't call that fear, pastor. I'm just wiser now and know where that kind of success can lead."

"No, Sam. You know where it led *before*. You are afraid to dream of being a successful foreman and builder again. You're afraid to dream of owning your own company and hiring your own foremen."

"And if I did dream those dreams again, why would it be different this time? Such ambitions ruined me," Sam said defensively.

"Because *you* are different."

Sam shook his head wearily. "To dream those types of dreams is too dangerous for me."

"You are afraid."

Sam sighed deeply. "I am not prepared to follow such dreams again."

"Not prepared how? Spiritually? Physically? Mentally?" asked Pastor Wright.

"I'm not prepared to handle the financial responsibility. I'm afraid that I would fall back into emptiness if I—" Sam stopped mid sentence. He leaned back and closed his eyes. Finally he sat back up and looked at the pastor. "You're right. I am afraid."

"Sam, this is great to hear. I know it sounds strange, but you are now ready to learn the sixth law of true prosperity—the *Law of Preparation*. And I believe deep down you know you are ready to once again dream."

Sam searched the pastor's face. "But I am safe now. I am content. I know where I was, and I like where I am now better. I know I am walking with God and following Him to the best of my ability. Yes, I know there are seven laws, but surely a simple man such as I am will do well to work and live by the first five."

"You were not born to be safe, Sam. You can indeed live a good life with honor by following the first five laws. You can be content and do a fair job no matter what your job title is or how much money you bring in. I agree with that. But, Sam, there is so much more to living a life grounded in God. Jesus died for your sins so you can experience so much more! You're not here to be a simple man who lives and works righteously but is afraid to dream. No, you're here to bring honor to the God who created you and designed you for a specific purpose."

Pastor Wright paused to slather some butter on a biscuit and take a bite. "Sam, when you use the talents God gives you to the full extent possible, you honor Him and you honor the life He gave you. When your life is totally dedicated to Him, you are willing to follow His leading even when it feels dangerous. I've found that following Jesus usually includes taking risks and stepping out boldly when He leads. And when you follow Him with all your heart, success in many areas usually follows, including at work and financially. Prepare for success, Sam. There is no shame in dreaming and working toward greater goals when you are solidly grounded in God."

"I've prepared for success before, and look where it got me."

"No, Sam, you didn't prepare. You followed your heart, and you advanced in your work, but when success came you became paralyzed. And then your definition of success took over and led you down a destructive path. You didn't prepare for success because you hadn't established a plan based on God's leading and wisdom that included giving, spending, and saving habits that would hold true no matter what your income was. And then you stepped out and invested in people and projects without praying about it and consulting people steeped in God's wisdom who would be willing to pray for wisdom with you. You lost money, and you lost hope. Strange how those are so closely tied, eh?" Pastor Wright shot Sam an inquisitive-yet-wise glance.

"I'm giving now, and Suzette and I are reducing our spending."

"And those two things are very good. But the sixth law, the Law of Preparation, calls for going even further. It's wisely managing the resources God gives us to further His goals and purposes. It encourages us to live in a way that honors Christ and points people to Him. To accomplish this, Sam, you need to rediscover the fire within you to love and create and work the way God designed you to.

"You've discovered that bad money management can destroy dreams, even when they're inspired by God. But if you start now, regardless of what your current income is, and follow the simple steps of sound financial planning, you can dig yourself out of the hole you're in. And those good financial habits will stay with you while you once again pursue the life God planned for you. In your case, I believe He will once again put you in a leadership role in your trade."

"These financial planning steps are simple?" Sam asked cautiously.

Pastor Wright grinned. "Yes! It's a simple formula. All you have to do is *give* ten percent, *save* twenty percent, and *follow a budget* to live on the remainder. When you figure out a budget, you need to include expenses such as home repairs, livestock costs, tools for your business, unexpected illnesses and emergencies, schooling for your daughters, perhaps setting aside money for their weddings, and saving for your older years when you might want to slow down a bit at work and spend time enjoying your grandchildren."

"Wait!" Sam protested and held up his right hand. "The first part was straightforward, but the rest won't be easy to figure out."

"When you think about it, Sam, being proactive in handling your finances and planning a budget will lead to a much simpler and stress-free life than no planning and no formula. You already know how 'going with the flow' can lead to major problems. Unless you plan and prepare, you won't find lasting freedom. And that's what you want, isn't it, Sam? Less stress and more joy?"

"Of course, but—"

"You'll be amazed at how desiring freedom can be a great motivator for sticking to a plan. You are right in one respect. The process won't be pain free. Altering our lifestyles and how we spend money takes time and effort, but I know you can do it. And I know Suzette will be a willing and helpful partner in this regard."

"You're right about Suzette. She follows a budget she set up for the household expenses. I'm sure she'll welcome the Law of Preparation. But I'm not very good at planning and having the discipline to stick to a plan, pastor."

"If you were only preparing for a balanced budget, the steps might seem tedious and difficult," the pastor said. "But if you remember that you are preparing for a life of significance filled with loving your family, doing the work you enjoy, helping the community, and praising God, then setting up a financial plan won't seem so daunting. Implementing the formula—*give* ten percent, *save* twenty percent, and *follow a budget to live on the remainder*—will ultimately enable you to freely pursue all God has for you."

Sam's heart lightened, and his eyes sparkled. "Pastor, will you help Suzette and me work on these goals of planning and preparation? Do you really think I can once again dare to dream without fearing failure?"

"Well, Sam, you must prepare mentally and financially for setbacks too. There will always be some, and I know there are lean times in the construction business. But if you're seeking and following God, He will enable you to live with a joyful and fulfilled heart no matter what your circumstance. I believe with all my heart that you are on God's path and your heart is ready to see money as a tool instead of a goal."

Sam took a deep breath. "Pastor, please help me prepare for true prosperity. I do want to be foreman of my own crew again. And I do want to be in a position where I can offer my ideas, use my talents and skills, and encourage others to do their best work. I thoroughly enjoyed working with my own crew and pleasing my customers. I feel alive when I get to do that, and my family benefits from my positive outlook. I know leading a team brings greater risks along with the monetary rewards, but with God's help and your help, I'm willing to give it a try!"

"Praise to God!" Pastor Wright exclaimed. "What a gift you give me—to allow me to teach you. Helping people is my passion. Let me look at my schedule, and tomorrow after church we can set up when we'll meet. We'll divide our time between reading lessons and finances. Letters and figures! How great is that? We're setting out on a wonderful journey, my friend!"

Sam enthusiastically shook the pastor's hand as he stood up. He thanked him for being willing to help. "And now I must go see Geoffrey," Sam said.

"I know Geoffrey will help you. He and I, well, let's just say we've been teaching each other many things for a long time. He's a godly man. I'll see you tomorrow then."

And life moved forward...

Sam and Suzette worked out a fine deal with Geoffrey. The large house on Miller Street was sold to a pharmacist, and Sam and his family moved into the cottage at the town center. They sold off some furnishings and paid off most of the debts Sam had accumulated. After much discussion and a few family meetings, their three daughters became more agreeable to downsizing and sharing the limited space. It wasn't long before the delectable odors of gooseberry pies, vegetable stews, and fresh bread filled the cozy cottage and wafted out the windows into the marketplace.

Sam's life was again on track, but that didn't mean it was always easy. He'd been through many hardships, but he hadn't realized how difficult learning to read could be. Pastor Wright continued to encourage him by insisting that persevering would result in many blessings. Every Tuesday and Thursday at five o'clock Sam met with Pastor Wright for reading and discussion. After the reading portion, the pastor read aloud from the Scriptures and other texts. Together they discussed theology, philosophy, poetry, and the human condition. This encouraged Sam even more because he hungered to know more about Jesus and living for Him.

Once a week Sam and Suzette sat down together to review and revise their budget. They stuck to the formula Pastor Wright taught them: ten percent went to God's work, twenty percent went to savings, and the remaining seventy percent went toward living expenses. They found that creating a living expenses budget was difficult. And it was sometimes hard to put money into savings when there were bills to pay and groceries to buy. But they stayed with the plan.

Sam and Suzette were surprised to discover they could get by with less. When Sam was a foreman, they seemed to barely survive on ninety percent of their income, and now they were trying to live on seventy. And Sam was making less money too. How many times did Suzette and Sam yearn to buy a beautiful rug or piece of pottery, only to admit it would cut into their savings plan so they'd better pass up the deal? How many times did Suzette serve turnip soup because she refused to go over the allotted amount for groceries. Yes, it was hard to give up the little luxuries they'd grown accustomed to, such as having the milk delivered twice a week, but they did.

Sam and Suzette could have grumbled, yet they chose not to. Most days they cheerfully attended to their family and work. They felt rich in spirit and hope. After a few months, they found that their sacrifices and disciplined ways were resulting in more than just adhering to a good financial plan. They discovered the peace and freedom that comes from being satisfied with what they had and living within—actually below—their means. To their amazement, they found they could live on very little. They began to enthusiastically see money as a tool that could be controlled. And they were quickly realizing that paying down their debts was providing even more freedom to give generously to others.

And time passed by...

Sam continued to work with John the Elder, bringing home a crewman's pay and a great deal of optimism for the work he might do in the future. Marcus's house was completed, and within six months Marcus's wife was shooing baby goats out of her bountiful gardens. Building and repair projects kept John's crew busy, and the men whistled while they worked through the winter and the following summer.

Sam also prayed and planned with God for the future. The Holy Spirit assured him that God's plan for him would be overflowing with joy, so Sam once again dreamed of becoming a foreman...and even owning his own company.

13
An Unexpected Problem

Sam stood with Grecco in the shade of a generous oak tree a year after Sam had been assigned to John the Elder's crew.

"I've been watching you, Sam," Grecco said. "Your workmanship is excellent, your attitude is right on target, and your dedication to quality is very apparent. John the Elder has repeatedly expressed his satisfaction with your work. He says you're a gifted builder and godly leader. He's asked me several times why I haven't promoted you again to foreman of your own crew."

Sam looked at Grecco. "Grecco, I'm eager to lead a crew once more. I'm sure I'm ready."

Grecco put a hand on Sam's shoulder. "I understand. I've been watching and noticing more than just your work. Your heart is renewed. I've heard of your generous support for the church and community. I know of your studies. I've seen how you've become disciplined and thrifty when it comes to finances and possessions. I've been impressed with your new attention to expenses on the job too. I need a man like you to lead one of my crews."

"I am ready!" Sam reiterated. "I realize at first jobs may be slow coming in. I'm prepared for that because Suzette and I have been putting some money away in hopes this opportunity would come."

"That won't be necessary. You can continue to work on John's crew between your foreman assignments. That is, if you're willing to be foreman and crewman at the same time." Grecco eyed Sam. "Would you have a problem with that?"

Sam smiled. "God's unfailing grace fills my life and my heart. I'm glad to do to the best of my ability whatever work I'm offered. Going from foreman to crewman between jobs won't be a problem at all."

And so Sam once again was leading a crew—a small crew, yes, but it was a new beginning. They were initially assigned to minor projects and repair jobs. The crewmen quickly became accustomed to and appreciated Sam's approach on each job. Roofs were thatched, stonework was laid, building frames were anchored, and drainage tiles were repaired with careful attention to detail and love for the customers whose lives would be touched by the work.

Between assignments, Sam worked diligently for John, accepting his instructions and insights with grace and a coachable spirit. John's best wishes for Sam came true. His work as a crewman quickly drew to a close as more customers requested Sam's crew and more men asked to work for him.

By this time, Sam and Suzette's goals and budgeting habits were well in place, and following their godly priorities was almost second nature. As Sam's pay increased, their giving and savings increased and their faith and dedication to God grew. Although they were still careful with their money, Sam encouraged Suzette to accept some small luxuries, so eventually they had their milk and cheese delivered to the house, ate more fresh fruits, and occasionally enjoyed dining out at a fine restaurant.

Sam found life invigorating. He looked forward to work every day. And his crew did too, which was quite a testament to Sam's leadership. The men knew their work was important, and they would be encouraged to do their best. After all, they were part of Sam's crew.

As Sam and Suzette's daughters grew up, Suzette's sewing

business gradually increased. Although her needlework kept her very busy, Suzette continued to teach the children to read at the church school. Martha, Elizabeth, and Mary—Sam and Suzette's daughters—were helpful students and happy learners.

Sam continued to be an ardent student of God's Word. Energized, enthusiastic, and spiritually and emotionally at peace, he explored the Scriptures and discussed what he discovered with Pastor Wright.

Yes, life was very good.

Until one day…

Sam arrived at Geoffrey's office with the mortgage payment and a smile.

The moneylender greeted him warmly before motioning for him to step inside. "I have an important matter to discuss with you, Sam."

"Of course, Geoffrey," Sam said, his brow furrowing slightly.

The two men sat down at a table in the small conference room, a pot of tea between them. In the quiet, austere room, Geoffrey's soft words seemed to boom like thunder. "Sam, you're a builder—a good builder. But there is something you've built that is wearing away bit by bit. It is crumbling and disappearing even as we sit here. I'm afraid it will collapse quickly if you don't take care of it right away."

"What are you talking about, Geoffrey? If I've done something wrong or not up to standard, please tell me so I can make it right. I don't want to disappoint Grecco or those who give me the privilege to build for them." Sam searched his mind quickly. *Have I constructed anything for Geoffrey lately? Is there a fence or wall that needed repair that my crew handled? Is there something else?* "Geoffrey, please explain, and I will fix whatever it is."

"I'm speaking of your savings," Geoffrey said with a slight smile.

Sam blinked at Geoffrey. Finally a smile played across the builder's face. "You are a good and thoughtful man, Geoffrey, and perhaps a little bit of a jokester, yes?"

"Guilty as charged," Geoffrey admitted. "But I am serious about talking to you about your savings."

"I appreciate your concern, Geoffrey. But Suzette and I have been very frugal, and we've managed to save quite a bit. You needn't worry about us. For the past year we've followed the path to true prosperity by tithing ten percent, saving twenty percent, and living on the rest. We've gotten out of debt except for the small amount we owe on our mortgage. And we're doing as you suggested by giving beyond our tithe amount to help people in need. We love being generous with what God has generously given us. So there is no danger of our finances going to ruin as they did before."

Geoffrey listened quietly, nodding with approval. "You've been very wise indeed. And so you and Suzette are feeling financially solid now?"

"I still don't earn what I once did, but yes, I am richly blessed. My strength is God's grace and wisdom, and my priorities are spiritually guided. I've been faithful to the laws of true prosperity, Geoffrey. I am blessed to share what Jesus has freely and generously given me, and now I can't imagine living any other way."

"It is wonderful that God blesses us so we can be part of blessing others, isn't it?"

"Absolutely! Suzette and I are committed to following God's path in every way possible. We are always learning more about living for Him, of course, but we are filled with awe for what He's allowing us to do. And we thank you too, Geoffrey, for helping to open our eyes and hearts to being more generous."

"God opened your eyes and hearts and made you generous people. He just allowed me to be one of the messengers. He prepared your hearts so you were ready to hear His wisdom."

"He always seems to know when I'm ready for the next step," Sam added humbly. "He opened my ears so now I put the love His Holy Spirit placed in my heart into my work. I study His Word by listening to the pastor's teachings, and I'm learning to read the Bible. I also pray, seeking understanding so I'll be ready to face the challenges life brings. And when it comes to money, Suzette and I have been good stewards and built up four thousand royal coins in our savings account. So you see, Geoffrey, life is going well and our finances are in great shape."

"But there is more to do, my good man. Tell me, do you know how much a pound of tea cost a year ago?"

"I couldn't say for sure," Sam said.

"Around sixteen farthings. How about a cord of good firewood?"

"Last year? About eleven farthings," Sam said quickly.

"And this year?"

"About eleven and a half farthings."

"I bought tea yesterday at close to seventeen farthings a pound," Geoffrey said with a groan.

"Yes, this is what happens. Each year costs go up a little. But wages usually go up too, so the extra expense has no great effect, true?" Sam offered casually.

"It has an effect to be sure." Geoffrey poured two cups of tea. "If you had eleven hundred farthings last year, Sam, and you bought ten cords of firewood to store in your shed, how much would it be worth today?"

"If the wood was kept dry, I could sell it for today's price. Eleven and half a cord, so eleven hundred fifty farthings."

"And would you have made a profit?"

"Not really," said Sam. "That eleven-fifty wouldn't buy any more goods today than my eleven hundred farthings would have purchased last year. Is that your point?"

"Yes. Good job, Sam. Now let's say that last year you didn't buy wood with your eleven hundred farthings. Let's say that, instead, you saved it in the bank."

"Then I would have made money because the bank pays three percent annual interest on my deposits."

"And after a year that would be…"

Sam did some fast figuring. "Eleven hundred thirty-three farthings at the end of one year."

"And if you were to take that saved money out, could you buy ten cords of wood at today's price?"

"I wouldn't have quite enough. My money would have—"

"Lost value, Sam."

Sam's eyes narrowed as he took this in. "My four thousand coins…"

"Will be worth less in a year. The prices of goods have been going up about five percent a year for as long as I've been tracking them. Some items go down in cost, but that is rare. That means you need a five-percent increase in salary after taxes every year just to stay even. And money in savings needs to earn five percent after taxes just to maintain its value."

"That's not good. The bank only pays three percent, so my money lost two percent of its value this year. But surely that's better than storing the money in my house where it wouldn't earn any interest at all," Sam said thoughtfully.

"To be sure, my good man. And you do need to be saving money. The twenty percent you put aside is wise according to the Law of Preparation. But if you keep your savings in a three-percent interest-bearing account, it slowly erodes over time. At the end of twenty-five years, when you want to use your savings for retirement or other activities, the account will have grown, yes, but it will have also lost real value because of taxes and prices that have probably increased faster than the interest rates. That means you're saving money, but you aren't *preserving* money. Do you see the difference?"

"Yes, and I find this disheartening. What can I do? Most banks don't pay that kind of interest on savings accounts."

"Since you've accumulated enough money in your savings account to cover emergencies and unexpected expenses, it's time to consider investing some of it. Investing opens the door to the possibility of earning five percent or more after taxes so your money maintains its value or even increases."

"No, Geoffrey." Sam leaned back. "I invested in several different accounts a few years ago, and I lost money. The business representatives promised huge returns, and I believed them. But the businesses I invested in failed, and my money disappeared with them."

"Yes, that can happen," said Geoffrey. "That's why it's important to be cautious and evaluate investment opportunities carefully. Some investments are less risky than others. As a moneylender, this is my area of expertise. It is my business to know how to get money working so it increases in value. If you'll let me, I'll be happy to guide you. Money well invested can grow, which means it's actually working for you."

Sam sipped his tea. He looked at Geoffrey and shook his head. "Investments are risky. I'm not sure investing is necessary because I'm content with what I have even if it doesn't keep up with inflation."

At this, Geoffrey leaned back, smiled at Sam, and then began to chuckle.

Sam was surprised. He'd never heard Geoffrey laugh.

"Sam, earning a higher return and preserving or even increasing your wealth doesn't make you greedy. Greed speaks to motive, to wanting more for more's sake. Seeking the best return on your money to preserve or increase it isn't being greedy. Let's consider some examples.

"If Martha wanted to go to school to become a teacher, would you consider it greedy to arrange for a higher return on your savings so you could afford to help her pay for classes at a university?"

"I suppose not," Sam said carefully.

"Would you consider it greedy to seek the best return on your money in case something happened to you so that Suzette and your daughters would have more funds at their disposal?"

Sam frowned as he considered Geoffrey's point. "So you're saying that some investments might reflect being a good steward of the resources God has given me."

"Yes. I know you're not a greedy man, Sam. If you were, I wouldn't be sharing tea with you on this fine autumn day and offering to help you protect your crumbling savings. I have little patience for greedy people." Geoffrey paused to sip his tea. "I understand greed very well, my friend, because once upon a time making money any way possible was all I cared about."

"Really?" Sam asked in surprise.

Then Geoffrey shared how he'd grown up in a poor household with a yearning in his heart for a better life. He discovered at a fairly young age that he had a gift for reading people and evaluating businesses, handling money, and parlaying money into more. He tapped into this gift wholeheartedly by checking out people, products, and businesses with the potential to grow. Then he invested in the ones he believed would flourish. As profits rolled in, Geoffrey attracted the attention of people who wanted to know the secrets to his success. Soon he was charging fees for giving advice on investments or investing money on their behalf for a commission.

Watching money turn into more money became an obsession. Every working hour was spent studying and graphing various markets and the prices of wheat, chickens, wool, and other commodities. He continually sought information from experts in weather, temperature, astronomy, geology, and other fields that could estimate or predict what would happen to crops and businesses. He also consulted with people who studied trends to see how people were spending their money—specifically what they were buying.

Anything that would help him make more money was fair game. He studied the progress of the king's projects, the royal court's wants and needs, and even the taxes that would be paid. Everything, he discovered, affected the prices and value of the various commodities.

When a fire raged through a forest in a distant area of the realm, Geoffrey didn't care about the people or the damage. Instead, he stockpiled local lumber so he could sell it at a premium the following season. When the king doubled taxes to build new roads, Geoffrey pulled his investment from the town's main jewelry business and paid cut-rate prices for gems, gold, and silver from people who needed quick cash. He sent these goods to foreign countries to be sold at great profit.

Geoffrey's business was earning money so he could earn more money. Although he made sure his business endeavors were always legal, he seldom considered how his practices might hurt others. Making money could certainly be done, and it could certainly be done well. Even bankers sought Geoffrey's advice and, after a while, Geoffrey realized he had more to gain monetarily by refusing to divulge his knowledge and plans and actions. Instead he created an investment firm and offered people opportunities to invest with him. He would charge borrowers or companies twelve percent interest and turn over six percent to those who secured their money with him. His assets and material wealth increased substantially.

When markets and opportunities flattened, he turned to lending money for mortgages and businesses even if he thought they might fail. He figured as long as payments were made he'd earn interest. If the payments couldn't be made, he'd take control of the collateral at a bargain price. The effects on the people involved weren't his concern. The objective was to make money, nothing more.

"For twenty-five years," Geoffrey recounted, "my methods

earned me a great deal of money. But in the process I became an empty man. I lost my passion and grew bored. To fill the emptiness inside me, I charged the highest rates I could—what the market would bear, as they say—to add the thrill of risk. I cared little about the borrowers' motives or whether they truly had the means to pay." Geoffrey paused and looked with humility at Sam. "I'm sorry to say that I loaned you the money for the house on Miller Street even though I knew you were in over your head. I thank God for helping me see my sin and then helping me to change."

Sam listened transfixed. He knew Geoffrey was a man of means because he was a moneylender. So why were his office and office furnishings so modest? Hesitantly he asked, "Did you lose a lot of money? I mean, what changed? Why did you change?"

"I had dealings with a man named Menro."

"I know him!" Sam sat up. "I stayed in his stables when I first came to town—eighteen long years ago. And last year I saw him in town." Sam paused to remember. "He told me to go see Magowin when I told him I was on my way to see you about a loan."

"He's a reserved man, that Menro." Geoffrey smiled. "Rarely in town, you know. When I met him he appeared to be a man of moderate means. He would stop in to make payments on loans for others, several accounts at one time. I assumed he was serving as agent in some way or perhaps was a moneylender himself. I dismissed him for the most part until I learned he wasn't a middleman after all. I discovered he was generously giving his time and talents to help folks who were having a difficult time meeting their financial obligations. I then incorrectly figured he must be a foolish man who wasted his money paying off other people's loans.

"When he arrived one day, I asked him about his motives. His reply stunned me. He said it wasn't his money he was using. That the money had, indeed, come from the borrowers. He met with them twice a month as a group, held discussions about handling money, and then collected their payments to bring to me. They were his students, he said. He was teaching them the way to true prosperity—giving to God, saving, budgeting, and investing. He was helping them partner with God to become disciplined. Many had taken second jobs, and some had sold possessions to pay down their loans. They were all determined to honor their obligations though.

"I asked him why he was helping them. He said, 'Because I love them, and God loves them, and they need help. And now they are becoming the most prosperous people in town. They will bless this town beyond measure.' I didn't understand, so I just stared at him for a long time. Finally I told him I had more wealth than all of them combined. Then Menro really shocked me. He said, 'No, Geoffrey. You are one of the poorest people in town. You may have lots of material wealth, but your heart is empty.' I should have laughed and sent him on his way, but he spoke with such compassion that I was intrigued. I asked him what he meant." Geoffrey smiled at Sam. "And I'm sure I don't need to tell you more, eh? I know Magowin has been working with you on the seven laws of true prosperity."

Sam was astonished. "You changed your view from this one conversation?"

Geoffrey chuckled again. "Oh my no. For a full year Menro talked with me. Every time he brought in the payments he shared his views on prosperity and how it was all about riches and not about material wealth and money. I also came to know Magowin and Pastor Wright. I'd known who they were, of course, but we weren't friends. They also shared about true prosperity every chance they had. Unfortunately, I was a hard case, so it took a lot of time before my heart thawed and I was able to hear the godly wisdom they were sharing. Finally God got through to my heart and my mind and my soul. I realized He had a far better plan for my life, and that He'd given me my talents to help others. I finally understood that I was wasting precious time by being obsessed with money."

"So you learned the laws of true prosperity from Menro, Magowin, and Pastor Wright? That must have been intense!" Sam said with a knowing grin.

"Yes, I did, and yes, it was. And since I know you've been following that path too, I knew you'd understand. That's why I brought up investing. I believe you're ready to learn the seventh law—the *Law of Preservation.* The gifts God has blessed me with tie into this seventh law. If you'll let me, I'd be delighted to encourage you and Suzette to be even better stewards of the money God has blessed you with by preserving it and, hopefully, watching your investments grow. That way you and Suzette will be in a position to generously help even more people in Jesus' name."

Sam took a deep breath. "Okay. Please tell me more about this Law of Preservation."

"The Law of Preservation is about finances, yes, but it's also about the other areas of your life. Achieving true prosperity involves valuing and preserving what's important, including your relationship with God, your health, your marriage, your relationships with your daughters and other family members, friendships, integrity in your work, the traditions that are important to you, the beauty and resources of God's mighty creation, and so on. Anything of value to you that you don't work to preserve will slowly fade away until it disappears."

"That's a long list, Geoffrey. Where would I even start?"

"Since my God-given gifts involve handling money, I will help you in that area. You will work on the other areas as God brings them up, okay?"

"That seems logical."

"For our purposes, the seventh law is about preserving the power and usefulness of your money by investing it. Money that is 'stored' serves one purpose only—a short-term resource for emergencies or unexpected needs. As we talked about, stored money isn't being preserved because its value erodes over time. Since we want to be good caretakers of the resources God entrusts to us, we need to ask Him for guidance and then put our money to work for His purposes, yes?"

"That certainly ties in with the other laws of true prosperity," Sam observed.

"To get the full value from our money and put it to good use, we need to be careful and wise. The most important starting point is to pray, asking God to guide you. The next step is to find a financial adviser whom you trust and who follows God and His principles. Ask him or her to help you. You'll also begin tracking funds and markets."

"That sounds difficult and time consuming. I'm not sure I have the time or energy," Sam admitted.

"You'll learn, and in a short time you'll become quite adept at tracking and managing your investments."

"So what do I need to start?"

Geoffrey smiled broadly. "You need a surplus of savings in the bank, which you and Suzette have. You will need to set a time when you and Suzette can meet with a financial adviser. And then you will need that adviser, which you have if you'll allow me to help you…"

"Yes! Consider yourself hired. I'll need to talk with Suzette, of course, but I'm sure she'll agree this is a good plan. We're going to become investors—a counseled investor, this time! Just like the wealthy have!"

"You are already a wealthy man, Sam, rich beyond mere material wealth. Now, before you go help me finish this tea. After all," Geoffrey added with a wink, "it cost me almost seventeen farthings a pound."

"Magowin, you look as though you married a fine cook!" Sam said after he stepped into the cobbler's shop and hugged his old teacher.

"Ho ho, my friend! You have a mischievous look in your eye. What have you been up to? Having a discussion with Pastor Wright? Wait, you haven't come to recite fancy poetry to me, have you?" Magowin stepped back and peered over his spectacles at Sam.

"I'll leave that to Pastor Wright," Sam said with a laugh. "No, I've just come from Geoffrey's."

"Ah, our soft-spoken friend. He forgets that I'm hard of hearing, but I love him just the same."

"He is soft-spoken, but I heard every word he said to me. He's agreed to counsel Suzette and me in setting up some investments."

"Ah, the seventh law—the Law of Preservation." Magowin's merry face broke into a wide, exuberant smile as he clapped Sam on the back. "You will do fine! And Geoffrey will help so you can enjoy watching your money grow. Did he tell you there is much more to this law than preserving money?"

"Yes, he did," Sam affirmed.

"In time God will let you know when you'll deal with the other aspects. Just follow Him and follow your heart, and you will know what you are called upon to leave for the generations that will follow us."

"Such grand words, Magowin! Surely a man such as I have little to offer the next generation, and any generations that follow."

"A man such as you..." Magowin looked at Sam with great affection. "A man such as you can share your faith and create a path that people can follow to find hope and true prosperity."

14
Looking to the Future

"Sam, I have wonderful news!" exclaimed Suzette when Sam walked into their cozy cottage.

"I also have news," announced Sam. "But I'll listen to yours first. What is this news?"

"I've found an apprentice!"

Sam paused. "An apprentice?"

"Yes! I've been praying and praying the right person would come along. Her name is Netta. She's thirteen. Her mother and father run the mill at the northern bend of the river."

"I know of them. Fine people. And this girl…?"

"Her mother came in the other day and showed me Netta's embroidery work. It was beautiful, Sam. She created the designs, and every detail was exquisite. It almost brought tears to my eyes. To be so talented at such a young age…" Suzette stopped to catch her breath and calm her excitement. "Her mom said Netta loved doing needlework and asked if she would see if I needed an assistant. So her mom came today to ask if I would be willing to take Netta on as an apprentice. I hesitated at first because she's so young, but when I saw her work I knew my prayers had been answered."

"You have been praying about this? And you say *I* keep secrets!"

Sam said good-naturedly. Then he smiled and hugged his beam-ing wife.

"I know, Sam. I've been meaning to talk to you about it, but we've both been so busy. I've had this dream of passing on my ideas, my skills, and the love and respect I have for my craft. Even though our girls are fine seamstresses, none of them seem passionate about needlecraft so I've kept my desire buried inside. I could scarcely utter this dream to myself, I wished it so much.

"I believe with the right encouragement and training Netta will be an excellent apprentice who will care as much as I do about the quality of the work we'll produce. And I'm excited about training a young woman who has great talent. I'll get to share with her the need to add love to her talent. This work I do will be carried on. It will be carried on!" Suzette's eyes glistened with tears of joy.

Sam listened and understood. "This is indeed wonderful news."

"Of course, this will mean that I'll bring in less income at first, since I'll be paying Netta some wages. And at first the amount of work I do will decrease as I spend time teaching her. In time, how-ever, I'll be able to take more orders. Together Netta and I will build this business. She wants to learn everything, from the books, to the customers' needs, to the purchasing of supplies. Oh, Sam, I've looked forward to something like this for so long!"

"Think nothing of the money, Suzette. We've managed on less, so we know we can accomplish anything. Plus, I'm earning more now and have bright prospects. This is a worthy undertaking. I have complete faith in your decisions and dreams. God is smiling, and you will be blessed by this."

"So many plans to make! I must prepare an area for Netta. We have such a small room available, but we'll make do. Sam, you said you also have something to tell me. What is your news?"

"Well, it's not as exciting as yours, but Geoffrey has asked that we sit down with him and plan out how we want to invest some of our savings."

Suzette stared at Sam. "Invest? I'm not sure we should risk putting any of our savings into investments. What if we lose money? Can't we just keep things as they are?"

"Then it will never grow, Suzette. This won't be like before. We won't invest in risky ventures. I have more respect for our money than that. But we do need to put some of it to work. We've got to or it will sit in a bank benefiting no one—not even us. We won't choose investments we both don't agree on. And Geoffrey will help us; he'll advise us."

"Geoffrey? But he's in the business of lending money to people in need. Why should we trust him to work toward our staying *out* of debt?"

Sam smiled and then he explained all that Geoffrey had shared with him.

Suzette listened and finally said quietly, "First, let's pray and give thanks to God for these new blessings. Then we'll talk about a good time to go see Geoffrey."

With Geoffrey's guidance, Sam and Suzette began investing. They kept a reserve of 3,600 gold coins in the bank, enough to cover six-month's worth of necessities, as Geoffrey advised. After a long session of questions, answers, and instructions, they placed the remaining 400 coins into four different investment accounts.

"Why four?" Suzette asked.

"Would you want to rely on orders from only one customer all year, Suzette?" Geoffrey asked.

"No. I need a range of customers to ensure I have steady work."

"Ah, the same is true with investing. There will be times when one market or one fund of money is less profitable, but the others will be making money. You serve your money well by allowing it to take part in a variety of markets. Diversity is the key to being comfortable with your investments."

Sam and Suzette learned that there was a wide variety of options—with varying degrees of risk and earnings potential. "This one fund I recommend," Geoffrey noted, "the one invested in grocers around the shire, this goes up in value more slowly than the others, but every three months it will pay you a dividend—a small share of the profits—much like receiving interest from the bank."

"Wonderful!" exclaimed Sam and Suzette.

Geoffrey put up his hand in caution. "Yes, but the wise plan is to ask that this small dividend be reinvested into more stock. This way you earn dividends on your dividends. Your earnings are compounded, and your overall return is higher. Plus…" Geoffrey smiled. "This is a disciplined way to approach dividends. Until you need income from your investments, why not put them to work for you too?"

And so they did. Every week they continued to put twenty percent of their earnings into the bank for emergencies and unexpected bills. At the end of each month they left 3,600 gold pieces in the bank and took the surplus to Geoffrey to invest into their four accounts. Every three months their dividends were reinvested. And slowly their money grew, building upon itself and helping to support and build other businesses, services, and new ideas.

Sam rebuilt his life on a firm foundation with sound cornerstones using the best quality building blocks. His income wasn't always the same each month, depending on the contracts he garnered, but how he handled those earnings was always the same.

After she took Netta under her wing, Suzette's income was less for quite a while. But she was overjoyed with the growth and preservation of the integrity of her craft. She delighted in mentoring this young person to carry on her workmanship and business practices, including putting love and integrity in every stitch. She was investing in another person so that together they would someday work in partnership to serve a broader base of customers.

Sam's building commissions grew steadily, and Grecco's faith in him solidified. After working full-time as a foreman for several years and handling larger and more demanding projects, Grecco chose Sam to head the entire guild operation, placing him over every foreman and every project. Sam's organizational and budgeting skills, his ingenuity and foresight, and his management style made him a wise and enthusiastic leader. His dedication to God and his sincere love for the people on his crews and in the town were apparent to everyone he worked and socialized with. His stellar reputation grew throughout the kingdom.

The town and realm were flourishing, and Sam and Suzette's investments grew and flowed through the business community. Although a few luxuries were added here and there, their basic lifestyle remained the same even though their financial wealth was growing under their wise financial care and Geoffrey's advice. When storms devastated a section of town, Sam and Suzette gladly donated money to help rebuild it. *What a blessing to be able to do so,* they thought. When Netta's father suffered a severe accident, Sam and Suzette sent for the best physician and paid the bill. They were overjoyed that God had blessed them so they could bless others. When Martha expressed a desire to attend the women's teaching college in the next town, Sam and Suzette had the resources to pay the tuition, provide funds for her weekly room and board, and cover her transportation costs home and back on the weekends. They made sure Martha knew God had provided the bounty they were using to help her.

Sam and Suzette remained in their cozy cottage, but they did add two extra rooms, to the delight of their daughters still at home. They created the comfortable, warm, inviting place with lovely things to lift their spirits and fine books and food to feed their souls and bodies Suzette had dreamed about for years. Although life still had its ups and downs, overall Sam and Suzette knew they were being blessed by the God they loved and served wholeheartedly.

One day the king decreed that he was looking for someone with a wise and steady mind to chair a planning commission to oversee the development of the many growing towns in the kingdom. "I want someone who is wise and has integrity and honor," announced the king.

"We know a man who fits that description," said many church leaders.

"I want someone who follows God, and who knows how to set and follow priorities," the king proclaimed.

"We know of such a person," said many of the business leaders.

"I want someone who has a genuine love and concern for my people. I want someone who isn't interested in lining his own pockets," the king stated.

"We know such a one," said many laborers.

"I want someone who generously gives to others," the king said. "Who gives of his time and energy."

"We know of such a man," said many of the townspeople.

"I want a man who knows how to study and understands how to apply what he's learned," announced the king.

"We know of a citizen like that," said many of the people on town councils.

"I want someone who is adept at planning and budgeting; someone who avoids debt and lavish spending," declared the king.

"We know just the person," said many Builder Guild members.

"I want a man who will preserve what is good in these towns, who knows the value of investing, and who considers the future while planning today's course," the king announced.

"I know just the person you're looking for," said Geoffrey during a private meeting with the king.

"Bring him to me!" commanded the king.

Thus it came about that a wood gatherer from the forest was placed in charge of gathering the best and brightest thinkers, planners, and builders in the realm to set a course for their growing communities. From business professionals to college students, from parents to single adults, from teens to the elderly, Sam brought together a variety of views to help establish prudent procedures and guidelines for developing strong communities and a strong kingdom. They also held town meetings where opinions, ideas, and suggestions were encouraged.

Bridges, aqueducts, town squares, marketplaces, and roads were designed and constructed or repaired and rebuilt. Woodlands, meadows, and forests were set aside as wildlife preserves and parks. Areas for farming were established according to terrain, irrigation, and accessibility. Several towns combined their efforts on similar projects—a revolutionary idea that saved money and reduced taxes.

Sam appointed Marcus as the committee liaison to the king to communicate the committee's suggestions for promoting citizen involvement and investment in the communities. The king encouraged his subjects to participate and provided several incentives. For instance, people who donated their time, energy, and supplies to school and church projects received credit vouchers for their taxes.

Sam was excited about this new opportunity to interact with other community leaders and citizenry. He gladly shared his time and knowledge, and yet he never forgot to make God and his family his top priorities. Whenever possible, Suzette and their two girls who still lived at home traveled with him. And Sam took every opportunity possible to meet privately with people to share the goodness of the gospel.

Sam considered his life full and satisfying. He was rich beyond measure.

15
Full Circle

A silver-haired gentleman wearing a green wool coat stopped by to see Sam in his office at the new town hall.

"I've come to see you because I am a concerned citizen," he told Sam.

"Menro! What a wonderful surprise!" Sam got up, walked around his desk, and shook hands with his old friend. "It's so good to see you. Please sit down and share what's on your mind. How may I help?"

"I'm concerned because we have a resource that has been decreasing in value for generations. A valuable component of our kingdom has yet to become part of the prosperity so many people are experiencing today. A group of us have been meeting, and we believe we must reach out and invest in this neglected resource. We are missing out on so much by not incorporating the available resources in improving our kingdom."

Sam listened intently as the man explained.

"Menro, two times you have spoken wisely to me. More than twenty years ago you helped me realize the importance of integrity and doing my very best at anything I set my hand and mind to. Ten years ago you directed me to a shoe cobbler to help set my feet on the path to real prosperity through knowing Jesus Christ as Lord and Savior and following His principles. Tell me what you speak of now, for I know your judgment and heart are true."

"Sam, I'm speaking of our brothers and sisters who live in the forest."

Sam was silent for a long time. Finally he let out a big sigh. "I know of these people, Menro. Often I have thought of them. My parents have long since passed on, but there are many who remain and come to my mind from time to time. I've never forgotten where I came from and how good the people in my village are." He looked at his refined friend. With sorrow and regret he added, "And yours is a noble heart to consider them. But these people care nothing for our carriage roads, brick buildings, aqueducts, and parks. Although not a contented people, they are resigned to their lot and choose to stay that way. In an odd way they take pride in their poverty. I know their ways and their thoughts. They will not want to join us townsfolk in bettering the kingdom, I assure you. They have no dreams…no hope…no interest in investing in anyone or anything outside their village. They have no love for us, Menro."

Undeterred, Menro spoke with quiet authority. "It makes no difference that they have no love for us. God loves them, and so must we if we're truly God's children. If they do not care for great buildings, that's okay. But let's clear a wide swath through the forest edge, and build a well-built, paved trail from their village to our town. That will let them know we're interested in them and that we want to know them. Let us then send people to teach them, minister to them, and support them. Let us give them opportunities to help us too and contribute to our community. We are missing a great opportunity to invest our resources and time in them. And God will bless our efforts, I'm sure."

Sam frowned, deep in thought. "You make some good points, Menro. And I do care about these people in my old village."

"And perhaps you're right, Sam. They may choose not to accept our fellowship. But maybe they will. And if even one person desires to reach out, to participate, to let us help him or her...or he or she helps us, hope and goodwill may be born. Perhaps one person in pain will accept our medical help and find relief. Perhaps one young person with a calling—with ideas that have been carefully hidden—will welcome the chance to talk to someone who encourages him or her to reach out and make a difference. And, Sam, perhaps there is a young man like another young man I once knew, who was a good wood gatherer but dreamed of creating an even better life and doing his best. This is a project worthy of our time and effort. It will be a very good investment for our town and for the kingdom."

The heart of a simple wood gatherer heard these wise words, and they resounded deep within him. Sam knew his friend was right. "Menro, thank you for bringing this to my attention. You have brought an idea that will not only help the kingdom, but it will give me an opportunity to give back to my home village. I will set the wheels in motion if you will agree to spearhead the project. We'll need a wise representative with a good heart to visit the village and share our love and hope. Someone who can help prepare the way for a friendlier, more supportive relationship between our communities." Sam stood up and shook Menro's hand. "Come, my friend. We have a new trail of hope and love to begin."

The 7 Laws of True Prosperity

1. *The Law of Wisdom:* Highest wisdom resides in God's supreme thought and love.

2. *The Law of Priority:* Success that matters and lasts can only be achieved when one prioritizes in accordance with divine instruction—at all levels, including financial matters.

3. *The Law of Motive:* Meaningful work and living are motivated by unconditional love for God and others.

4. *The Law of Generosity:* Service, caring, and giving create abundance, for others and ourselves.

5. *The Law of Understanding:* To love with God's heart, see through His eyes, and think His thoughts are the ultimate goals of true disciples of Christ.

6. *The Law of Preparation:* Being responsible with and wisely managing God-given life resources requires commitment to truly important purpose and careful planning.

7. *The Law of Preservation:* Wise stewardship of God-given resources ensures that money, principles, values, and spiritual guidance can be passed from one generation to the next.

About the Author

Cecil Kemp Jr. and his wife, Patty, have been married for more than 40 years. They enjoy spending time with their two children and four grandchildren.

A CPA, Cecil has worked as a chief financial officer and as a chief operating officer for publicly and privately held buisnesses. Cecil and Patty have also owned and operated many successful businesses.

As a result of lessons learned from Cecil's near fatal accident in 1993 and the unexpected death of his father in 1995, the Kemps sold their businesses and have focused their energy full-time on The Wisdom Company—an umbrella organization that oversees their writing; inspirational speaking; life, financial, and business coaching services; and their DifferenceMaker brand, which includes "The DifferenceMaker: Online Radio Show" and DifferenceMaker Leadership Institutes, Clubs, and Rallies.

To learn more about the Kemps, their ministries, resources available, The Wisdom Company, and the DifferenceMaker brand, visit their website: http://www.difference-maker.net.

More Books by Cecil Kemp

Supernatural Living
4 Steps to Achieving Real Success!

The Secret Meeting Place

Wisdom & Money
Applying the 7 Laws of True Prosperity to
Make the Most of Your Money

Wisdom, Honor & Hope
The Inner Path to True Greatness

The Hope Collection
(beautiful, full-color gift books)

A Book of Hope after Retirement
The Best Years Are Ahead

A Book of Hope for a Better Life
Inspiration Today from Reflecting Back & Looking Within

A Book of Hope for Achieving True Greatness
26 Keys to Highest & Lasting Success

A Book of Hope for Higher Connection
Truth, Inspiration & Wisdom for the Searching Soul

A Book of Hope for Lasting Peace
Inspiring Thoughts for Possessing Real Hope & Security

A Book of Hope for Leaders
86 Day Guidebook to Leadership Greatness

A Book of Hope for Loving Unconditionally
The Power & Passion for Living Life Fully

A Book of Hope for Mothers
Celebrate the Joy of Children

A Book of Hope for Parents
Inspiration & Wisdom for Successful Parenting

A Book of Hope for Relationship Heartaches
Wisdom & Inspiration for Mending Broken Hearts

A Book of Hope for Shaping a Life of Honor
How to Live a Life of True Excellence

A Book of Hope for Students
Dream Big, Dream Wisely!

A Book of Hope for the Storms of Life
Healing Words for Troubled Times

A Book of Hope on Abiding Faith
Rediscovering the Rock of a Meaningful Life

A Book of Hope on Prayer
Key to Successful Days, Lock of Secure Nights

A Book of Hope We're Forgiven
The Healing Power of Forgiveness